15 of the 16 DUMBEST THINGS
I Have Ever Done in an Airplane
AND WHY!

RICHARD TAYLOR

15 Of The 16 Dumbest Things
I Have Ever Done In an Airplane
and Why!

© 2023 Richard L. Taylor, Jr.

ISBN 13: 978-0-9987528-2-2

All Rights Reserved. No part of this book may be reproduced, stored in a retrieval system, or transmitted in any form or by any means without written permission of the author.

Full Quark Press
112 Krog Street, Suite 196
Atlanta, GA 30307

Copy Editing by Candace Johnson
Proof Editing by David Kaufman
Interior Layout by Jera Publishing
Cover design by Richard Taylor

CONTENTS

Flight Plan 1
1 A License to Learn 7
2 You Can Never Share "Alone" 21
3 How to Fly a Deck Chair Home 43
4 'Tis a Fool's Errand That Seeks a Bridge Too Far 73
5 Zero-Zero 93
6 Back-Seat Driver 105
7 Open-Door Policy 115
8 Schrödingers' Flip-Flop 123
9 Taildragger 137
10 The Iceman Cometh 147
11 "Roll The Pole" 157
12 "Glacier Girl" 171
13 The Missing Man 189
14 DC-3, P I C 203
15 You Haven't Failed Until You Quit 217

Photo Credits: 229

"just doodlin', Boss…"

FLIGHT PLAN

FIFTEEN OF THE sixteen dumbest things I have done in an airplane, you ask? Come on now.

Don't let the title fool you. Sure, at first blush this statement almost sounds like I've only made sixteen dumb aviation missteps. The truth is, I am just like all the other pilots you know out there. My actual whacky-number eclipses sixteen by an embarrassingly large *multiplier*. Although I've never done anything as dumb as run out of gas, one time I did try to taxi out of an aircraft parking area with one wing still firmly anchored to a tie-down ring. Another time I landed at a wrong airport, but that wasn't entirely my fault. Thankfully, I've never neglected to put the wheels down before landing – and that's good. But there was that time I did not latch the cabin door properly before takeoff. Technically, this issue wasn't dumb, it was just carelessness. But still, my solution to this particular door problem might be considered a little iffy. See Chapter 7.

I don't know whether jumping out of a perfectly good C-119 Flying Boxcar in full combat gear was dumb or not, but my fire-breathing Jumpmaster didn't give a rat's ass what I thought. We were over the Drop Zone, and the little green jump-light on the door jamb just started blinking, and he was ready for all 40 of his Airborne *grunts* to "un-ass this great aluminum bird" – *and right now*! I was first *in the Stick* so out the door I went. "Hup thousand, two thousand, three thousand …" At four thousand, your chute's supposed to pop open. You'd be surprised how only four seconds can morph into a lifetime of thinking about the dumbest things you've ever done in an airplane.

SP-3 Richard Taylor, Germany, 1957
11th Airborne Infantry Division

As with most pilots, I really do have way too many truly embarrassingly *dumb stories* to share with anyone, except, you guessed it – a good shrink.

Speaking of which, somewhere along the line I did go to one. We discussed a lot of things, but none of them had the first thing to do with aviation. They all had to do with, well – you know – *whatever*. Anyway, at the end of the last session, she said something like, "Yes, Richard, you do have a little problem. But to fix it, all you need to do is just *shorten your string* a little bit. If you can do that, you'll probably be okay." Obviously, it had to be good advice because I didn't really understand what she meant by *shortening my string*. As she was carefully laying out her thesis of *my problem* to me, of course I was doing exactly what everyone else does in a situation like this. I was animating the images of her discourse with that mental projector inside the forehead and just above the eyes. The mental image I created at this de-briefing was displayed as a very large, gas-powered, industrial-grade, long-stringed Weedwhacker loudly chomping-up anything that got in its path. But as you've already guessed; I was seeing mostly what I wanted to see and thinking mostly what I wanted to think. The big difference this time was that my interpretive image of what she was saying had now armed me with *my* own personal Weedwhacker metaphor. I would now use it for all my future lapses of acceptable behavior. All brains work this way, don't they?

To one degree or another, the fifteen chapters in this book are episodes of aerial activity that sometimes fall outside the established boundaries of everyday private and commercial aviation protocol. Obviously, many pilots have looped and rolled general aviation airplanes – or flown them from the back seat by shifting their weight side to side – or they've made zero-zero visibility landings or flown under a bridge or two. With the exceptions of Rolling the Pole and extracting a World War II fighter plane from the Greenland ice cap, (and maybe the execution of a barrel-roll while flying blind in the clouds), all of the antics in the following pages have been performed before by many general aviation pilots. But even so, at the very least, they are infrequently revisited.

The intent of my writing about questionable comportment here is not to glorify incorrigible behavior. It's the opposite. I try to

15 of the 16 Dumbest Things I Have Ever Done in an Airplane

explain some of the physical and/or psychological circumstances that may provoke what are sometimes perceived as "roads less traveled by."

In general, I think we can agree that *all pilots* enjoy bragging-rights concerning certain moments of aerial challenges of daring-do. This is a privilege that simply comes with the territory. But they are also, to one degree or another, admissions to testing the boundaries of established decorum. Judicial prudence might suggest simply stuffing any out-of-step flying adventure under a pillow somewhere, and then sharing with friends only the emotional satisfaction of making a perfect instrument approach in legal, but minimum, weather conditions without violating any established boundaries whatsoever. Even though such an event might be an incredible source of personal satisfaction – one that is almost beyond description to one who hasn't tried it – most of us can only appreciate never-stepping-out-of-bounds for only so long. But that still doesn't mean that it's a virtue. I submit that it means wayward end-use behavior deserves the scrutiny of an eye that can also see beyond the prescriptions of strict-rote-behavior.

It is in this broader context that I share the 15 experiences offered herein. But even if some of these events are wrongly inspired, if they are neither recorded and shared, their value (good or bad) will eventually evaporate by normal half-life decay, in which universal *good* will not be fully appreciated, and universal *shame* will not be reprehensible.

Hmm. This is starting to sound a little bit like that long-string Weedwhacker image that Dr. Shrink didn't know I assigned to her final dissertation on my *issues*. (She never actually mentioned the words *string* or *weedwhacker*. That was me trying breath some visual life into her learned but lackluster appraisal of some of my discordant issues.)

Flight Plan

So, before all this stuff gets too heavy, let's go ahead and file our Flight Plan, buckle up, take off and have some fun. I hope you enjoy the ride as much as I enjoy sharing it.

FLIGHT PLAN

Type:	Thoughtful/Personal
Destination:	Undetermined
Departure time:	Now
Route of Flight:	15 Waypoints
Pilot's Name	Richard Taylor
Souls on Board (SOB)	2 SOBs (just you & me)

CHAPTER 1

A License to Learn

TWO WEEKS AFTER finishing college in Atlanta, I landed a full-time, paid position as a draftsman in one of the highly-respected architectural firms in Atlanta. With my tee-square in hand and slide rule worn in a leather scabbard on my belt like the M-1 bayonet I wore in the Army; I was ready to take on the world. The starting salary was a shade above that of an entry-level rough carpenter – $3.75/hr. The job was not only intellectually challenging, it was steady income with paid-overtime. Thus began my 3-year internship to be an architect.

I was also ready for those *flying lessons* that I held out as the carrot-on-a-string for myself to finish college.

My first solo flight took place at Gunn Field, Georgia, on February 13, 1965. Hence forth, the concept of "pilot" was pressure-embossed on my soul for its remaining duration.

Gunn Field is gone now. The relic of its less-than-a-wingspan wide runway is now invisibly intermeshed in a suburban subdivision. But back in the mid-sixties, some 20 air miles due east of Atlanta, it was a beehive of activity hidden off a county road in the slowly domesticating boondocks of rural Georgia.

Its physical presence back then was anchored by a small, one-room, un-air-conditioned, unpainted, wood-framed house barely repurposed as an aviation hub. In the central room was a thread-worn sofa, a few straight-backed chairs, a coffee table, an old wooden teacher's desk with a rickety-based swivel chair, a blackboard for ground-school lift/drag diagrams, and a large-scale aviation chart of the State of Georgia stapled to the wall. On it was a weighted string affixed to the airfield location and threaded through an eyebolt at the top of the map. A hand-lettered, distance-measuring scale was laid out horizontally from the fixed end of the string to offer distances from the airport. It didn't take but a few seconds to figure out how to use it.

Abutting the rear of the building was a sometimes-less-than-antiseptic unisex convenience. The most memorable quote on its graffiti wall was, "A man's ambition is pretty small if he writes his name on a shithouse wall." It was neither signed nor dated.

Gunn's 1500-foot-long landing strip ran east–west only a hundred feet or so south of the office's front door. The undulating topographic contours of the runway faithfully followed the somewhat assertive natural rolls of the local terrain. West was uphill. The sloping grade of the strip was helpful when taking off to the east because the downhill run would accelerate the plane sufficiently to get airborne before the end of the runway. Consequently, in only a light breeze, planes frequently took off in one direction and landed in the opposite. It took a little experience before a student pilot could be confident in judging whether it was the wind or the terrain that controlled the direction of the landing pattern. I must note here that aviation subtleties like this are seldom addressed in the big, expensive flight schools more convenient to metropolitan areas.

Some of those *big airports*, as we called them then, even had control towers with radio communication, level runways with lights, and well-maintained, gender-specific toilet facilities. A few even had pilot bars where the rigors of an afternoon of *touch-and-goes* could be shared with other pilots, young and old. After an afternoon of flying lessons at Gunn, there was only the forty-five-minute, nose to tail, Interstate drive on I-20 back to the ground-hugging, herd-mentality of urban civilization.

Because of the absence of runway lights, night training was not part of the flight curriculum at Gunn. Quite fairly, of course, the educational opportunity offered at urban airports was generously reflected in the cost per hour of flight time. For those of us with the skinniest wallets, Gunn's *affordability factor* was what made this whole flying opportunity possible.

All of this is to say, the flight instruction program here focused more on the fine art of fundamental aircraft control and manipulation, rather than high-tech, electronic communication and sophisticated navigation training.

It took me two months to scrape together enough cash to pay for the 9.5 flight hours it took me to solo (fly without an instructor). But man, was I ever hooked!

It then took only a few more hours for it to become eminently obvious that *real pilots* fly their own airplanes.

Two more months later, now with a total of twenty-two flying hours in my logbook, but with steady employment, I floated a bank loan and bought an almost-worn-out, 4-seat Cessna 172 for $5500. That was twice as much as a new 4-door Ford Fairlane cost back then. Tie-down space at Gunn was dirt cheap, so that's where I berthed her.

GUNN FIELD, JUNE 1965

Seeking New Horizons?

A few months later, on June 16 (now with forty hours in my logbook), I passed my FAA check ride and became a freshly minted, fully licensed *private pilot* – with his own airplane! Finally, I was cleared to "shed the surly bonds of Earth … and touch the face of God."[1]

This was the magic I had dreamed about since those adolescent years of sniffing the dope that I was frugally applying to the rubber band-powered paper and balsa fighter planes during World War II.

One week after my check ride, I buckled into my now freshly scrubbed and polished Cessna 172, (call sign, N6247E), and flew

---
[1] "High Flight" by John Gillespie Magee

A License to Learn

her from Gunn Field up to DC, and landed at Washington National Airport, right there on the Virginia side of the Potomac River. I had a total of 46.5 hours of flying time. My flight instructor at Gunn told me several times that to land at the big airports, when you're still 15 miles out, all you had to do was call the control tower on the radio and they'd tell you exactly what to do next. The tower radio frequencies were printed somewhere on the aviation charts. He said that the best way to learn to use the radio was simply fly into the big airports like you own them. What can be easier than that? Besides I had used a Walkie Talkie in the Army! I was on my way.

The Cessna had only one radio, a Narco Omnigator Mark II. It possessed a dozen or so different transmitting crystals (frequencies) and a vacuum-tube radio receiver. You operated the receiver dial with a small rotating crank-handle like the one on an old pencil sharpener. To pick up a station, you rotated the crank, and the little vertical receiver dial would go back and forth. The speaker would go *weeoouuo* until it hit a station and you could hear a voice. Obviously, it could only catch a station-signal while that station was transmitting. Sometimes you had to ask the person on the other end to give you a *short count* (count from one to five and back). This would give you a few seconds to tune them in. A *long count* was from one to ten and back. All of that drill is only for the receiver side of the radio. The transmitter side of the radio was operated with a separate clicker-selector knob. The radio would transmit on a selected fixed crystal frequency and receive on the tunable *weeooeeo* variable frequency. This old-timey technology was called *duplexing*. Because of its charming little receiver crank, the radio was affectionally named a "coffee grinder."

With all this electronic wizardry at hand, it never occurred to me that I wasn't a handsome airline captain flying a mighty four-engine, triple-tailed Lockheed Constellation with seventy

15 OF THE 16 DUMBEST THINGS I HAVE EVER DONE IN AN AIRPLANE

admiring passengers in the back. I even practiced deepening my voice when I called anybody on the radio and said, "Roger all Charlie. Over." (I think "Charlie" is old military code for "information." But I'm still not sure.)

A year or so later, I was still getting the hang of navigation and communication and needed to go to New York City to visit my wife, Lucy. She moved up there from Atlanta some months earlier to accept a highfalutin' executive-level position with a large and prestigious international accounting company. Our six-year marriage had been an exciting experiment, but not one made in heaven. It was one made by two energetic and ambitious young people, each hell-bent on finding and building themselves into something different from what they were when they fell in love in high school. One of them was educated, sophisticated, articulate, smart, and beautiful. The other was a Korean War Vet with a duffle bag still stuffed mostly with personal barriers. Holding hands with someone you grew up with, while pursuing different life-goals, can be challenging. Even though this thumbnail sketch is brief and unfinished, it probably sums things up close enough. So, let's just leave it at that.

The primary purpose of this upcoming weekend visit was to finalize the details of our divorce agreement. In other words, my eagerness to get to the *Big City* was very much like the weather my trusty old Cessna and I were about to challenge: i.e., uncertainty laced with *guilt, shame* and boundless personal *hazard*.

Atlanta to New York is a long haul in a little airplane – some 800 miles, in fact. Late Friday morning, I took off downhill from Gunn Field with broken overcast and headed northeast. Of course, the weather gradually worsened the farther north I flew. I didn't know enough about radio procedures to *duplex* ahead for current weather conditions. Only recently had I learned to say "Roger" instead of "Okay" to a control tower.

A License to Learn

I refueled at a little airfield near Richmond, Virginia at sunset. When I got to the Chesapeake Bay area, it was totally dark. I should have found a place to spend the night, but target fixation took over and I just kept going north.

The engine roar in the old Cessna was always substantial. At night, it's worse. The next two and a half after-dark hours were spent in light rain mixed with roaring solitude. The overcast continued to lower and gradually compressed available altitude down to 2000 feet.

It seemed to take forever, but the first glimmers of Manhattan finally started to radiate off the overcast cloud immediately ahead. Oh, man! I cannot begin to express what seeing that glow meant to me, except that it was a sense of joy still mixed with generous amounts of uncertainty, ignorance and anxiety – all of which is a big improvement over the immediately preceding hours of very nervous gloom.

I eased over to the right of the skyscrapers to fly up the East River. With a flashlight in my mouth, and scaling distances off my chart with the ruler, LaGuardia should be 7 or 8 miles on the other side of the Queensboro Bridge. The left fuel tank had run dry back around Philadelphia. The right tank now indicated only a quarter-full. I calculated that this gave me something like thirty or forty minutes of flying time left. Keeping the million lights of Manhattan Island on my left-front and Brooklyn's almost-million on my right, my path was a pitch-black-run up the East River. This would lead me, I hoped, to my destination. The bottom surface of the overcast just above my head continued reflecting the gentle luminosity of the city. Then, rather quickly, right in front of me, like an internally illuminated pearl necklace, Queensboro Bridge turned up about where I hoped it would. The red lights atop the proud support towers were in dazzling contrast to all of the dense glitter of white lights blanketing *urbanity-personified*. The river system below, of course, was still the ink-black highway guiding me north. Identifying the bridge was a huge relief. However, I still couldn't find the alternating green and white flashing control tower light used to find airports at night. Whether I could actually see it or not, it was now time to call LaGuardia (LGA) Tower and announce my arrival. Maybe they could help me find them.

Because I was unfamiliar with all that highfalutin approach control protocol, I skipped them and just called the tower directly. They didn't even flinch at my lack of radio etiquette and immediately assigned me an altitude of 3,000 feet. Then they radioed me again, "Four-seven-echo, call the airport in sight." The base of the overcast in this area was about 2,500 feet above the ground with light rain. Obediently, I pulled the control wheel back and climbed up into the cloud base to get to the assigned altitude. Of course, I also immediately lost all visual connection with everything outside the cockpit. This was my first actual experience in "flying blind." This means flying only on instruments. That this happened on a dark, rainy night didn't help. *Dark* immediately took on a new dimension of isolation.

Sometimes, if you're lucky, circumstances accelerate learning curves. Without asking permission, I pushed the nose of the plane over and dropped back down *out of the clouds* to 2,400 feet. It then took a few more seconds for me to get all the 45-degree angled buildings on Manhattan Island to go back to their vertical position. Man, oh man! Being in that cloud for less than a minute was a life-lesson on where you never want to be.

I then leveled out at an altitude to just skim along the bottom of the overcast cloud base.

Except for maintaining the assigned altitude, I obeyed all of my directional instructions faithfully. But I still couldn't find the airport. Trying to help me out, the tower then gave me a new heading and asked if I could "see the rabbit lights at twelve o'clock." Did he say *rabbit lights*? What the hell is that?

As professionally as I could, I answered, "Negative." I forgot to include my call sign, but they didn't seem to notice. The tower then said they would turn the runway lights up to full-bright and then blink them off and on.

Holy shit! The airport was right under my nose, and not even a mile away! The tower was talking to other on-frequency, commercial aircraft about a *light aircraft* doing something. I was too excited with the runway lights to follow their conversation. Besides, they weren't talking *to* me – they were talking *about* me. On top of that, they were talking too fast for me to even butt in. But I did anyway. I broke right into their rapid-fire business chatter and told the tower, "Four-seven-echo has the runway in sight!" Without hesitation, they answered right back with the magic words, "Cessna four-seven-echo, cleared to land Runway Four."

That moment, right there, was when that *small airport* training at Gunn Field earned its keep. I was well practiced at dropping this plane like a quarter in a slot machine. This "short runway" at LGA was four times the length of Gunn Field. I pulled the carburetor heat control on, pulled the power full back to idle-cutoff, lowered the flaps all 40 degrees in one smooth action, then dropped the left wing with hard opposite rudder and slipped the plane sideways right in. Because the plane does a little falling-leaf action in a full-slip with full flaps, using that last 10 degrees of flaps is controversial. But I'd practiced it several times, and I promise you that the plane feels like you're falling sideways, vertically down an invisible tube. We touched down before the midway point of Runway Four.

The landing was damn near flawless. But before I rolled to a stop, the tower told me to switch to the Ground Control frequency. Ground then directed me to follow the blue taxiway lights to the general aviation operation at the southwest corner of the field. Their last transmission instructed me to telephone the control tower immediately after I checked in at the service desk. I deep-voiced, "Roger."

After I stepped out of the plane and without locking the cabin doors, I went into the general aviation lobby and walked right past the service counter to the men's room. Finally, I had a few moments to gather my thoughts. I then washed my hands and walked straight out through the terminal's main lobby entrance doors, stepped into the first-in-line taxicab, and politely asked the driver if he would take me to Manhattan. I had left my travel bag in the plane, but right now, I had a whole lot on my mind and figured I'd face whatever aviation discussions the tower wanted to have when I returned here the day after tomorrow – Sunday. At this particular moment in my life, I simply needed mental breathing room.

Naturally, the couple of days with my soon-to-be ex-wife, were letter-perfect. Things always work this way. I slept on the couch, and Saturday we went to the Metropolitan Museum of Art, then to dinner at a deli and then to an off-Broadway play that night. We were both on our best company behavior. Precious memories and practiced civility can turn the poisoned thorns of a failed marriage of dear friends into living theater.

At the crack of dawn Sunday morning, and after a kiss on a dearly familiar cheek, a sincere brotherly hug, and a *thank you* for letting me use an old, worn-out toothbrush, I caught a taxi back to LaGuardia. For Lucy and me, this was the new start we both needed. With unfaltering respect for one another, each of us then went our separate way to begin the rest of our lives. Our friendship never wavered. Nonetheless, at that moment, my heart was simultaneously agonizingly empty and painfully overflowing with both guilt and relief for what felt like several levels of conflicting emotional upheaval. But they might not have been conflicting. They might have been working in harmony, but in different musical keys. Who knows?

But without question, Sunday morning still offered me a witch's brew of guilt, crime and punishment, and aviation uncertainty.

Thankfully, the weather was not part of the brew. It was simply exquisite. Even the clear blue sky had a measurable tailwind component to it. In fact, it was way too nice for the belated telephone call I needed to make to Air Traffic authorities concerning that former life of mine. Hell, I knew I was wrong, stupid, and way over my head last Friday night. Consequently, this morning my brain was swirling with uncertain notions of the Cessna being impounded and me going to jail to await my hearing.

There was also another, pragmatic dimension of the return-home reality. The cost of the fuel to get to New York, the taxi fares, the modest meals and incidentals all dug deep into the paltry amount of cash I carried in my wallet. Of course, I didn't ask Lucy to pay for anything. Not eating today was a given – no big deal. But more important than my appetite was the serious question about whether I had enough cash to buy fuel to get all the way home. Even a modest twenty-five-dollar fine for not calling approach control would break the bank – a bank that was already broken.

When I got out of the taxi at the airport, I counted out the fare in pocket change and gave the driver a quarter tip. He just looked at me. After a direct trip to my favorite men's room to get my head straight, and without making eye contact with anyone in the general aviation lobby, I walked right past that same service desk and straight out onto the parking apron to my plane. Remember, I had no luggage.

Somebody had properly secured the plane with tie-down ropes. I performed the preflight ritual by slipping the tie-down knots, checking the oil, draining condensation from the fuel tanks, and walking around to look for anything unusual. The pilot door was still unlocked so I got in, turned on the master switch so I could test the stall-warning horn. I then made an instant decision to buckle the lap belt. Since nobody had come out after me yet, I turned the key on, yelled, "Clear" out the window, fired up the engine, taxied off the apron to a taxiway, looked both ways, gave it full throttle, and took off heading south down the East River right over the elegant Queensboro Bridge.

I made this departure before considering all the aviation protocols I was bypassing. Not only was I not the least bit proud of myself, I was bitterly ashamed. Whatever procedural infractions I incurred when I landed two days ago were now compounded exponentially. Still, they could all be addressed just as well in Atlanta as here. Besides, I wasn't certain that I had enough money to buy gas to get all of the way home anyway. Maybe I'd get lucky and run out of gas and crash and all this would just go away. A freshly hollowed-out heart sitting on top of a very empty stomach was about all I could take of the *Big City* right now.

If shame were a virtue, I'd be an archangel right now. But it isn't. And I'm not. I'm back to being a bucket of shame.

The plane, of course, had not been refueled. The left tank was still empty, and the other still indicated just shy of a quarter full. I selected the first small airport in New Jersey on my navigation chart and just hoped to high heaven they would be open early Sunday morning. They were and I filled up both tanks and had a few dollars left over. And no, I didn't buy even a Coke for nourishment. By loafing along at only 70 miles per hour and leaning the fuel mixture down to a gnat's ass, and *with that gentle little tailwind*, I made it to Greenville, South Carolina. With the balance of my pocket money, I bought eight and a half gallons of gas. It did not even fill one tank, but it got me back to Gunn Field, Georgia.

A License to Learn

As I share this journal entry of a young pilot's brazen disregard for regimen and order, I don't see even a thread of an admirable image in it. Not even close! I see a young man completely over his head in a series of potentially dangerous situations. So, he bumbled his way through. Big deal.

But the truth of the matter is, he isn't the most important character in this event. The real heart of this story is about that tower controller who, two days ago, guided an inept young pilot in a very dangerous situation to safety. More important, it's not what that controller saw or didn't see; *it's what he sensed.*

Let's think about it. Right at the height of a rainy, Friday night rush-hour at LaGuardia Airport, he had some little Cessna duplex in that he was in the neighborhood ready to land, but did not have the airport in sight. The Tower Controller did not simply close off the Cessna's approach as many (and maybe most) controllers would have done. He certainly had the authority to do that. But he sensed something else in this situation. He elected to squeeze in this lonely Cessna from who-knows-where. This was not just a perfunctory accommodation. I am convinced that he knew more about the situation than just my radar signature. Maybe he too had a divorce agreement discussion the night before, and what he needed right then was an impossible circumstance to bend his mind around. On the other hand, maybe he was a new hire with a superintendent watching over his shoulder, saying, "Okay, Jake. Let's see if you can work in this Cessna-hick during rush hour. He's either a newbie or a nutcase. I'm watching you, kid. I wanna see what you's made of. And you's better not screw up!"

Whatever the real situation was, in the heat of the moment, somebody else's initiative and incredible decision-making saved my bacon. This was a fact selfishly unrecognized in my initial storytelling of that landing at LGA that night. Nevertheless, it was the tower controller who made the life-saving decisions better and bolder than mine that night. And remember: after I landed, I didn't even return his call to say thank you. I still owe somebody, big time!

Now before I forget, I eventually did learn what *rabbit lights* are. They are those sequential, bright, blinking little things that can show even a dimly lit pilot at night where the approach end of a runway is. Live and learn.

One more thing. *Thank You, Jake, or whatever your name really is. You are cut from the fabric from which real heroes are crafted. I am eternally grateful to you.*

CHAPTER 2

You Can Never Share "Alone"

SEPTEMBER 16, 1969.

For the last fourteen months, I have been making a 200 mile, once-a-week flight from Atlanta to Savannah to attend to the creative hiccups of the construction of Oglethorpe Mall. This project is one of those big, regional, retail complexes with three big-box department stores as anchors, a movie theater and three enclosed, air-conditioned pedestrian malls connecting everything together. It is the largest and most audacious piece of architecture I have ever designed. Now in its construction phase, as one might expect, there are more than a few traces of overly ambitious design notions intersecting the brutal reality of actually assembling all the pieces in order.

Thankfully, however, Scott Hudgens, the owner/developer of this project, loves the design. So long as I attend to said hiccups, (ones I characterize to him as *alternate design opportunities),* with dispatch, he smiles and stays happy. This morning, I'm anxious to get into solving a handful of real-life, nuts-and-bolts issues. I can't wait to get there. Architecture, from the first free-hand, napkin-sketch to the final walk-through with the owner, is an incredible way to justify one's existence.

It's been four years since the LaGuardia episode. I now have more than 1000 hours of flight time and hold an instrument/ commercial pilot's rating, and fly a spiffy little Mooney, Super 21 out of Peachtree Airport. This facility is replete with a control tower, sophisticated radio communications, instrument approaches, long runways and a classic pilots' bar called The Downwind.

Before I left my treehouse this morning, I called the weather briefers at FAA Flight Service. They offered "PDK (Peachtree Airport) to remain low overcast in Atlanta, then clearing early afternoon. Savannah's forecast is 600 broken with winds southeast at seven. Chance of thunderstorms."

This sounds routine for September so I go ahead and file an instrument flight plan to depart at 0800.

Sketch to repaint for Mooney Super 21

I almost always take someone from my office with me on these junkets. It's a good chance to study who we are and what we do professionally. Today, however, everybody else is busy pursuing their own hiccups, and that's fine. Maybe it's even a relief. Solo cross-country flights offer a little quiet time to reflect on stuff. Naturally, if you're

You Can Never Share "Alone"

the introspective type, this is a special treat. But even if you're just a regular guy like the rest of us, it's still pretty good.

The flight plan calls for one hour plus thirty minutes en route. Within thirty seconds after liftoff, we tuck up into the underbelly of the low-slung overcast. The weather forecast called for solid clouds from Atlanta nearly to our destination. In other words, there will be no reference outside the plane to tell us which way we're going or even which way is up. Our well-being will be governed by blind obedience to a small grouping of instruments in the control panel right in front of my nose. Maintaining heading, altitude, and right-side-upness is accomplished by faithful compliance to the readings of four or five essential (but otherwise unalarming) gauges.

As one might guess, the altimeter takes care of altitude, the artificial horizon takes care of staying level, and the compass tells us which way to go. The turn-and-bank indicator and the airspeed indicator refine these movements. The other half-dozen instruments in the panel relate to fuel quantity and flow, engine oil pressure, and temps. When you throw in navigation and communication with air traffic controllers, (and no autopilot), there is usually enough going on to keep one mentally engaged.

For the next hour or so, the whole world will be no wider than two movie-theater seats sitting side-by-side without an armrest between them. The view beyond the windshield will be no more interesting than if it were a movie screen showing only that the projector light was inadvertently left on the *dim* setting. In other words, there doesn't seem to be much going on except whatever random notions run through your head.

After take-off, I maintain climb power until we reach our first assigned altitude of 3000 feet. Just as the altimeter needle touches that number, Peachtree Tower radios us that they are handing us over at Atlanta (ATL) Departure Control. I switch frequencies and dial them in. They clear us up to 7000 feet and instruct us to proceed to Savannah (SAV) by way of Dublin VOR. VORs are navigation beacons usually named for the closest town to their geographic location. For cross-country flying, one flies to one's destination simply by connecting the dots (VOR beacons).

Today, we have only one intermediary signal – Dublin. It's about halfway between ATL and SAV. Once you get the hang of this system, cross-country navigation is a hell of a lot easier than missing an interstate exit sign out of the corner of your eye because an eighteen-wheeler blocked your line of sight.

After I report crossing Dublin VOR, Atlanta Center hands us over to Jacksonville (JAX) Center. *Centers* control all the big areas between the approach and departure control zones that that are around the big commercial airports. Long distance air traffic between urban areas is not yet fully covered with radar surveillance. That service is some years in the future.

When JAX Center eventually hands us over to SAV Approach, we should be back within radar range of SAV Approach. They will then give us headings to steer us to their airport where we will then be handed over to the SAV Tower to land. That's when we throttle back, lower the flaps and landing gear, chirp the wheels on the runway, tie down the plane, catch a taxi to the hiccup-site, and turn back into real people with productive and purposeful missions in work-a-day life.

But we haven't gotten that far yet. We're still back in the otherworldly phase of the day's work – just dutifully plugging along in the deep belly of an endless cloud layer.

I radio JAX Center and tell them we're with them at 7000-feet. FAA protocol requires that pilots flying outside of anyone's radar range, tell the center when they cross a VOR, the aircraft altitude, and where they are going next. FAA keeps track of them by taking notes of these radio contacts. Keep in mind, this is 1969.

You Can Never Share "Alone"

The faithful four-cylinder Lycoming engine up front is humming along effortlessly. I inhale a big mouthful of this rare-air just to hold some of it inside me. Holding it, even for just a few seconds, synthesizes these moments into whoever it is you are ... or think you are ... or even who you want to be. But I'll tell you this: you can only get away with all of this stuff when you're alone. If you take a passenger, you're a tour director who has this annoying preoccupation of having to steer and talk on the radio. Nonetheless, flying is still a special treat to share with somebody. But you can never have it both ways. *No matter how hard you try, you can never share alone.*

So far this morning, the ride has been comfortable, with only a few intermittent undulations. Visibility remains zilch. Because neither puffy clouds nor glimpses of the earth below pass by the windows, there is absolutely no sensation of anything going on anywhere. In fact, it feels as though the world is stationary, and it is only other people's time out there somewhere that's moving. Well, that's not entirely true. There is an endless little stream of moisture droplets running jerky paths up the windshield. There is also the inaudible but resolute movement of the red second hand on the panel clock. As for anything else going on anywhere... *nada.*

About twenty minutes after reporting in over Dublin to JAX Center, the light-level in the plane dims a little. This is curious. My first thought is positive. Maybe this might be a little welcome relief to a totally uneventful flight. Coincidentally, however, the pleasant ride changes from the little corduroy ripples to actual bumpety-bumps.

It continues to get darker. Even though nothing identifiable is happening, I scoot my seat a couple of notches forward and, by reflex, cinch my lap belt a little tighter. The light level continues to decrease. Mental wheels start spooling up, but there is still no actionable response I can do about anything.

I check the clock – 8:56 a.m. Then, in my head, I rerun the weather report I received a couple of hours ago. At the very end of the briefing, I vaguely recall the words, "a chance of thunderstorms." Here in the Sunny South, thunderstorms are what everybody expects with late summer afternoon buildups. When that happens, they are dangerous and ugly, and all pilots make a big point to fly around them.

Even more vaguely, I recall something back in ground school about how some cold fronts can develop thermal convection cells. I'm starting to think maybe ...

Then, all hell breaks loose!

In that instant, what-ifs don't mean a damn thing anymore. The runny drizzle on the windshield is wiped clean by a torrential explosion of a fireman's hose at full blast. Water doesn't pummel the airplane; it mechanically hammers and beats it like a blacksmith forging a glowing horseshoe. The entire airframe shudders with its impact. The new roar easily drowns out the normally loud thrum of the engine.

Reflexively, I pull the throttle way back and pull back on the yoke to slow the plane down. A mist of filtered water and spray is now filling the *inside* of the cockpit. It must be coming through openings in the firewall between the instrument panel and the engine. Maybe it's coming from around the door seal or through the ventilation system. There is an acrid smell of fresh steam sizzling off the exhaust manifold of the engine. I don't know where the rest of the water is coming from, but the cabin upholstery is already wet. My eyeglasses mist over so quickly that I have to whip them off and stuff them in the corner of my open flight case on the seat next to me. I then shut off the ram-air intake to the engine and the ventilation system to the cabin. Right now, the intake manifold that brings in combustion air to the engine has got to be sucking in volumes of water. Even the fabric ceiling-liner above my head is misted wet.

Then, WHAM! Things get worse. Magnitudes worse!

The steady water-pounding is completely upstaged by a physical impact of a midair collision. My flight case slams into the headliner next to my head and then ricochets to the back of the plane somewhere. Charts, approach plates, calculators, pencils, and my back-up, handheld compass all scatter everywhere.

Then my business briefcase sails from the back seat forward – missing my head but hitting the windshield with great impact. The case stays latched and bounces around in the cockpit like kids batting a beach ball in the backseat of mom's car. Even with my seat belt now cinched down as tight as it will go, the up-and-down accelerations cause body-stretch that forces my head hard into the fuselage structure above the headliner.

To further reduce power, I try to bring my right hand down to the three engine control knobs. My hand won't go down! It's waving around like a rodeo rider coming out of the gate. Then inertial forces reverse, and that hand now involuntarily smacks down between the seats and instantly weighs a ton. My left hand maintains its death grip on the left handle of the control horns.

Reaching a radio knob to dial the emergency frequency is not possible. The selector knob is too all-over-the-place to catch. And even if I could grab it, I'd never be able to feel the clicks of rotation or even read the small numbers to make a 121.5 MHz EMERGENCY call. Informing the outside world about what's going on right now is not going to happen. The handheld mic on its spiral-coiled umbilical cord is bouncing all around the cockpit. Even if I could catch it, the compression and extensions of my chest prohibit speech. I can feel animal grunts in my chest at each reversal in pitch and altitude. Besides, I need both hands to try to control this thing. The noise level in the cockpit remains thunderous. But I hear none of it unless I think about it. My brain is being bombarded by many frantic, internal mental voices yelling impending doom.

The light level is now too dark to read any of the numbers on any of the gauges. Besides, they are jumping from eye level to belt-buckle height in split seconds. It continues to get darker. The electrical switch for the panel lights is at the bottom edge of the left-hand side of the instrument panel. There is no way I will let loose of either hand to flick it. My head continues to either sink into my chest or extend hard into the airframe above the headliner. The only geometric consistency right now is that the instrument panel is always going in the opposite direction from my head. Head up, panel down. Panel up, head down.

The turn-and-bank indicator needle in the panel goes so far beyond its limits that it's useless. The gyrocompass is also of no value. It is impossible to execute a turn in any direction or even to hold any semblance of a heading. The altimeter needle winds and unwinds like it's being operated by a broken main spring. Once or twice, I catch a glimpse of it, and we're thousands of feet above or below our assigned altitude. Sometimes with the control wheel pushed full forward and the engine at full throttle, the airspeed indicator still pegs at zero!

The airspeed indicator and the artificial horizon are the only gauges I watch. They show *how fast we're going* (or not) and *which way is up* (or not). With too much airspeed, either the wing spar will fail (or detach from the fuselage), or the ailerons, rudder, and/or elevator will be torn away. At what speed the windows blow out, who knows? But it probably doesn't make much difference anyway. One way or another, *this airplane is about to disassemble.* Right now, this is my only sense of certainty.

Reinforcing the physical conviction of this impending event are the frantic voices going on in my head. It's not the same chatter you get just doing something dangerous (or stupid). It is now a rabble-rousing hysteria of contradictory commands. No matter if they are driven by an emotional frenzy or just unvarnished fear, I know I must somehow separate myself from the paralyzing effect these internal voices are having on me.

The airspeed needle again pegs at zero. I push the controls full forward to pick up some speed. Again, even with *full push and full- power*, the nose will not go down. *A flat spin* flashes through my mind! I keep holding the controls in that position. The airspeed indicator does not respond. Then the plane suddenly drops farther, like we just fell through a hole in the bottom of another hole. Again, my head hits the ceiling, and the airspeed needle winds right back up past the redline. The NEVER EXCEED redline for this Mooney is 170 mph. I watch the indicator needle go up into the 230-mph range (the highest number on the dial is 180 mph. I later estimate the rest). I have already pulled the throttle back to idle-cutoff and hauled the nose up again to slow everything down. Except for still being here, there is no reasonable evidence of any success from any of my attempts to control this aircraft.

Throughout all this noise and fear, confusion continues smothering my brain. Inside my head are still the frantic voices of internal shouting. One howls, "This is how it happens!" Another is screaming, "The plane is coming apart!" And another yells, "Push it over!"

On another mental level, there is still that growing certainty that this uncontrolled flight will not last very much longer. It can't. Then, strangely, I get a flash of something relax inside my chest, something like *comfort* in this inevitability of these events.

Another thought then flashes through my head so quickly that I react before I can think through its consequences. It could have been a quiet voice. The maximum safe airspeed for extending the landing gear in this airplane is placarded at 120 mph. Mooney Corporation has calculated (or tested) that only bad things can happen with the wheels extended down in the slipstream above this speed. The airspeed indicator is still going so crazy that there is no way to know what our real airspeed is. But right now, that doesn't make a damn bit of difference. To slow things down, I've got to create some drag. With my right hand, I reach down between the two front seats and unlock the Johnson bar that mechanically operates the landing gear. Then I manually lower the wheels and lock them *in the down position*. Even if the wheel-well doors or the gear itself are torn off, that energy may help slow things down a little bit.

But now, with the gear fully extended, nothing slows down. This makes no sense. The new drag makes absolutely no discernible difference in either the aircraft handling or airspeed excursions. Even though it's now thunderstorm-dark in the cockpit, I can still see the airspeed needle go again above the 200 miles per hour range. We then hit a *wham*, and it goes straight down at *zero*. Something just came off the airplane!

It isn't flying. It's tumbling. I have no idea if we are going up or down. Then, faster than I can even think about getting the gear back up, the airspeed winds right back up again past redline – and that's exactly what the extended gear was supposed to help avoid! Yes, I know. The mechanics and physics of all this do not make aerodynamic sense. But I'm strapped in here watching it happen. Maybe it's needle-momentum or instrument aberrations caused by leaks or breaks in either the vacuum or pressure systems, or maybe there's water in the airspeed indicator system causing the instruments to go erratic. Maybe there are incredible air-pressure changes in a thunderstorm that render altimeters and airspeed indicators completely irrelevant? I don't know. But deadly speeds on the air speed indicator are what I'm looking at. Right or wrong, it's all I have to guide my actions.

Another thing comes to mind. I see no lightning. Either it doesn't happen in the microsecond I'm thinking about it, or this cell we're in hasn't matured to that stage yet. Is it possible that lightning forms only at the base of clouds that are maybe several thousands of feet below us? Or maybe I have completely zoned lightning events out of my thinking. None of this is anything I dwell on. They are only microbursts of thoughts no bigger than the period at the end of this sentence.

Aside from the incredible pandemonium going on both inside and outside the airplane, the most frightening aspect of this entire episode is still the frantic voice-chatter going on inside my head. At the very beginning of all this chaos, the internal voices contributed significantly by offering logical, diagnostic and analytical observations. That part was good. Even at the first impact of rain, the voices did okay. But when we hit the turbulence – the *wall of mortal inevitability* – the chatter rapidly shifted from thoughtful engagement to confusion *and self-destructiveness*. As I said, they ended up *yelling* all that, "this is how it happens" stuff.

Not well concealed in this statement is that the "it" is a reference to death. The mixed voices' chants of raw fear replaced the trusted problem-solving roles our inner voices are supposed to offer. Putting the gear down might be the only good idea they came up with. Beyond that, all their hysterical babble does nothing but fuel more confusion. Right now, as the predictable and terminal conclusion of all this chaos becomes ever more evident, incrementally, I accept that I must face up to *the inevitable*.

It is then, in a pause of futile exasperation, I simply think to myself, "Clear my head and steady my hand." I don't close my eyes. I don't say *please*. This is not a plea to God to alter the predictable circumstance I'm facing right now, nor is this any kind of request for salvation. Honestly, deep in my heart, I cannot imagine that God is much concerned one way or the other whether I live or die violently in this thunderstorm or peacefully when it's all over. My appeal (call it a prayer if you want) is neither pleading nor humble. It is simply a request for personal qualities that I am desperately short of. Maybe it's for mental strength and personal character. I don't know what it's called, but if granted, it can carry me right up to that event which I am convinced is only fractions of a moment away; an event that starts with the explosive burst of the plane coming apart ... the raging storm-tempest roaring in ... the blasting deluge of water ... the smell and taste of blood rushing to the sinuses ... the savage tearing of the engine from its motor-mounts, and the propeller wildly chewing up everything in its uncontrollable summersaults ... then the terrible and weightless spiraling down through the dark wet storm ... the breathless wait with clenched teeth for the final impact in the unmoving, indifferent earth below ... down there where impatient people might be huddled safely in their kitchens, watching weather reports on morning TV, waiting for the storm to pass so they can drive their pickups over to the convenience store to buy a fresh pack of smokes.

Maybe, by then, the storm will have spit me out as innocuously as you would a watermelon seed in a nicely groomed and rain-refreshed soybean field.

And that will be the simple ending of this brief story that will never be told.

But it hasn't happened yet.

What does happen is that in response to my request, the chatterbox voices all turn off like a tripped circuit breaker. Then another *Voice* transmits. This one is calm, clear and not hurried. It is not anyone I know and it has no accent. But it is a man's voice that is patient, confident and clear. It narrates in an emotionless pitch, step by step, exactly what I am supposed to do. I sense that it has neither motive nor agenda. It offers not the slightest hint of salvation. It only explains, in practiced, professorial diction, the appropriate procedure to handle this uncontrollable *and probably terminal* situation. It seeks neither my allegiance nor recognition. Most importantly, I have absolutely no feeling that it is here to save my ass. I think it is here only to help me finish this thing with a clear head and steady hand. And that is all I asked for.

The airspeed indicator needle again pegs on zero. With neither introduction nor emotion, the *Voice* says, "Push the nose over. Push it to the stop. Now ease the throttle full in – don't jam it. Keep your right hand on it. The prop and mixture controls will take care of themselves." The *Voice* does not mention the landing gear, and I don't bring it up. In fact, I don't talk at all. I'm just a mute equipment operator, and until I'm instructed otherwise, the wheels will stay down.

Even though the *Voice*'s prescribed procedure is exactly what I've been doing so far anyway, I know full well that the plane is still going to come apart. Nonetheless, the calm assurance of the *Voice* is compelling. In a way, I now feel exonerated from any responsibility concerning the outcome of this event.

I have no way of measuring how much time has passed since I entered this storm. Although it seems like forever, I wouldn't be surprised if it were not even a full minute.

But I do know this: the turbulence *does not* slacken in the least. The *Voice* does not part the heavens, and the sun does not shine. It's still dark as hell and as violent as when all this started. Again, my feeling is that the *Voice* controls only *my mind* – not the circumstances I'm in. But most importantly, I am no longer the subject of any of the hysterical chatter of the frenzied brain-demons. It's now just the two of us – the Voice and me.

For some reason, I feel that I am now protected, not from death, not even a little bit; but from *fear. I am offered nothing more than calm resolution to the inevitable.* Whatever happens from here on out, will just happen. I get to watch and do things. And if everything doesn't work out, my downside loss is that I won't get to tell anybody about all this voice-business. Judging from my new state of mind, apparently, I'm okay with that.

Time, of course, continues on without dimension. It is no longer ticking by. Maybe it even stops too. Now I have all the time in the world to ride this thing out. No longer is there any urgency to get out of this sticky situation, nor even to get it all over with. It's all still drama and I continue in my roles as equipment operator and court reporter.

When I made my open request for a quiet mind, for some reason (maybe just vanity), I also asked for a steady hand. I have to say, my hands were never shaking at any time, nor are they now. My guess is that the shaking-hand thing must have been metaphorical – perhaps having to do with the expression of fear. Maybe it's like the steady-eyed appraisal you might give all the ghoulish spectators looking up at you as the hangman snugs-up your thirteen-knotted noose. Obviously, I'm not entirely sure what was in my head when I asked for it. It has no practical value. Nonetheless, the physical assurance of steadiness came with the package.

Also of note, this new *Voice* is not making just a cameo appearance. It sticks around. Well, I think it does. Remember: time stopped. A lifetime can now be a split second, a minute, or eternity. It all has to do with the *speed of time*.

Every bit of the deadly dynamics inside this thunderstorm maintains its full vigor. I continue doing exactly what I've been doing – twisting, turning, pushing and pulling the controls way beyond design limits. The climatological fury continues unthwarted. But as I said, it no longer has any of that sense of threat it had before.

The timeless aspect of all this is especially important. It solves a world of problems. Its greatest virtue, I think, is that it eliminates any sense of urgency to get *it* all over with. But as I said, I'm now just along for the ride.

You Can Never Share "Alone"

Then, as I'm about to get comfortable with my new indifference to these crazy excursions of altitude and uncontrollable airspeed, out of the corner of my right eye, I think I see a flashbulb go off next to the wing-tip of the plane. Maybe it's that lightning I was looking for. But maybe it's ... I don't take my eyes off the panel for even an instant. I only study the blur of instruments. Peeking might be like seeking hope. There is no way I'm going to swap my newfound armor for something so pitifully fragile as *hope*.

Besides, idle rays of hope don't match up even a little bit with the gift of *spiritual security* I have been given.

Then, in just the briefest *whatever you call time without duration*, the flight controls connect up a few feelings of answerable response. I rolled the wings level and they started to move in that direction. The Mooney just wanted to fly like an airplane!

I'm not ready for this. And I especially don't want to let go of the *Voice*!

Then an indisputable brilliant flash just happened. The loud water-roar switches off. The dark water-curtains against the windshield just wash back to reveal a full-color, horizon-to-horizon, wide-screen rendition of a new full-color production of "Welcome Home to the Sunny South, Y'all."

I can almost hear a Dippity Disney overture!

Thousands of feet below us, scattered on an exaggerated National Geographic agrarian-green landscape, are loose scraps of scattered cloud-clutter. The rich blue sky above us comes right down to a clearly defined horizon. The Atlantic Ocean is in perfect focus 15 or 20 miles off to our two o'clock. I know this area. We're 30 or 40 miles off-course to the north of Savannah Airport.

I look left and right over my shoulders at the dark dragon's belly we just popped out of. In both directions, the ominous roiling gray/black granite clouds are extending out of sight. And yes, it all looks totally disinterested in either the soaking-wet Mooney or the raggedy-assed me. We are now just freshly discharged annoying waste substances who are now ready to go back to exploring the more pedestrian pursuits of mortal ambition. What an incredible demotion!

Simultaneously, the *Voice* goes silent. I cannot overstate its loss.

The Mooney hums along faithfully and I'm back to being just another wet-head guy in damp khakis and a mist-soaked turtleneck.

I take this reprieve-time (yes, time started ticking again) to compose myself before calling JAX Center. As crazy as it sounds, there is still something in me that doesn't want to let go of the whatever-it-was that we've just been through. A big part of me still wants the humble dependency to the *Voice*. Could you ever be lonelier than when you raise your arms to hit the finish line of your life, but then the rope disappears – and you've got to keep on running? You're not even a little bit winded, and you ask yourself, "why the hell do I still keep running?"

By tracing its spiral-coiled umbilical cord, I find the hand-mic to the radio under the copilot seat and try calling JAX Center. Both radios are stone-dead. Neither will either send nor receive. Nor will the navigation receivers' work. Obviously, everything got a serious soaking. Good! Returning to government control is a long way from where my brain wants to be right now. This new sunshiny morning with two hours of fuel left in the tanks, and neither radio nor navigation equipment operating, is a free pass to play the airplane game with ingenuity and creativity rather than by text book rules, habit and discipline. On top of that, if we finally do land at Savannah, doing so *incommunicado* will only add juice and dimension to an incredible event.

Finally, everything is going my way. Right now, I need to slow down, go back to paying attention to details, and not screw anything up with hair-brained notions of whim and fancy.

But, hold on! There's something bad-wrong with this airplane!

It's not flying right! It won't hold altitude without dialing in too much nose trim. The slipstream noise has a whistle in it, and the controls are sluggish. Also, the airspeed is indicating too slow for the power setting. We're also yawing left and right. This is serious. My *steady hand*, the one I asked for earlier but later said I didn't need, is still steady. My head is clear. Mentally, I'm easily on top of whatever happens next. I need not ask for anything.

My first speculation is that the problem is either a bent wing spar or a twisted rudder or elevator. Maybe one aileron pushrod is broken, but the other one is still working. Maybe it's a twisted fuselage or bent engine mounts changing the angle of thrust. To relieve structural stresses on the airframe, I gently ease the throttle back to an easy slow-cruise, but I don't give away an inch of altitude. I eventually get everything down to a nice and easy 80 miles per hour.

While we're burning off speed, I'm looking ahead for the largest flattish field without trees or fences within gliding distance. I'm also looking for smoke for wind direction, but find none. I trim the plane to where my touch on the controls is superlight. This way, whatever has gone awry is balanced, unstressed and maybe won't finish breaking or falling off completely.

Although this morning's adventures are not over yet, there is no remaining evidence of the previous personal brain clutter (fear and/or anxiety). The noisy chatter box voices are still back in the weather-front behind us. This is the way it's supposed to be.

A half mile to the left of the nose is a green, well-groomed field of low crops. If we need it, it's twice the area we'll need to land safely. I bank gently in that direction. This is putting money in the bank in case the best-guess investigation I'm about to undertake tells me to put this airplane down *right now*. Since the Mooney uses its wing-skin as its fuel tanks, I start sniffing for leaking gas. I also double-check the fuel gauges for evidence of a ruptured tank. No smells. And the tank quantities are both normal.

I then start the full diagnosis with gentle banks left and right so I can look behind us to see if we're trailing smoke, fuel or oil. Nothing is visible. Next, I start a visual scan from the very top of the instrument panel. The most prominent instrument warning light is at the top-middle of the panel. It's the landing gear warning light. And it's glowing bright green!

Green means: "The wheels are *down*, dummy!" (I added "dummy" because I forgot to retract the landing gear after we popped out of the bad weather). A flick of the Johnson bar and the gear tucks right back up in the wings, just like it's supposed to. No binding. No hesitation. I listen for whistling sounds from possibly bent gear doors, but everything sounds fine. No. Better than fine. I continue the sniff test. It stays negative. The old Lycoming keeps on humming its faithful song and never misses a beat. With the wheels up where they're supposed to be, the plane now trims up normally. I add power and we ease right back up to normal cruise speed. The pristine soybean field I just picked is saved from some goofy watermelon-seed story that nobody would ever really understand anyway.

I keep thinking. I am alive. I am alone. I am the most important singular event in an extraordinarily complex universe. Now how is that for unfettered ego and vanity?

My plan now is to visually follow the coastal highway down to the Savannah Airport. I'll then circle the tower, blink my landing lights (if they work) and have them welcome me aboard with a steady green light signaling that I am cleared to land. If the weather there turns out to be below visual flight rules (VFR), or if the plane doesn't feel right, I'll either break the rules and land there anyway, or I'll backtrack to a smaller, uncontrolled airport – maybe Hilton Head Island. I'll figure out the next step after I get to Savannah and read whatever light-signal they give me. Right now, however, I'm more than content to fly along lazily and not talk to anybody.

Well, damn! Wouldn't you know it? Number 2 radio just crackled back to life with all its familiar background static. I dial in Savannah Approach Control and receive them loud and clear. With my best measured radio voice, I tell them that we've been through a little weather and lost radio contact with JAX Center; and that I am now with Savannah at 7000 and 25 miles northwest of their airport. I don't want to get into the thunderstorm story with them. Apparently, however, they never missed us and/or weren't much interested anyway. Maybe we're that tree that fell in the forest that never made a sound.

Approach responds and clears us for the instrument glide slope (ILS) approach. Number 1 radio (which is still inoperative) has the plane's only Instrument Landing System receiver. I'm looking at the weather over in the airport's direction, and it looks more scattered than broken. Scattered has less cloud density than broken. Either way, a visual landing looks like a piece of cake. The fortune pendulum has swung all the way back our way, and it's now our turn to shine. I radio Approach, "Two Eight Yankee has the airport in sight." They hand us over to the tower and they clear us to land. The rest of the approach and touchdown are textbook.

I am now back on terra firma – still damp, but still breathing!

After parking the plane at the general aviation terminal, I find my glasses on the hat shelf behind the rear storage compartment behind the back seat. Before I walk over to the service counter to order fuel, arrange a tie-down for the day and call a taxi, I walk around the Mooney to look for any surface distortions like skin wrinkles or structural deformities.

I don't know what you call the thing I feel right now, but for sure, it is not one of those *aha* moments where the pilot kisses the spinner and names the plane after his mother. I would, however, be happy to just pick a June bug off the leading edge of the wing and flick it in the grass beyond the tarmac. But the plane is squeaky clean – pressure washed to perfection. Instead, I simply finish my inspection tour and walk through the lobby of the terminal and wait for my taxi. Corny or not, however, there really is a "we" connection in here somewhere. I just don't know how to describe it – or even do what you're supposed to do with it.

The day's work at the Oglethorpe Mall job site is pretty much what I had looked forward to. I make one everyday design decision right after the other – important things like relocating plumbing lines, solving air-conditioning–duct conflicts, selecting floor tile grout colors, and aiming accent lighting over the landscaped areas at the main mall intersections. But today, there is something different in this process. For some reason, each decision is disproportionately more important than if I had just shown up for work with a job to do. Today I'm aware of just being here.

At dusk, I'm back at the airport. Flight Service confirms that the cold front has now blown north past Atlanta and all the way to South Carolina. The current weather forecast calls for cooler temperatures and an unblemished night sky all the way home. The Mooney, acting like she didn't know all about my June bug comment this morning, fires up on her first compression stroke. Both fuel tanks are topped off with 100-octane. Yes, I crawl under the wings with a flashlight to check again for fuel leaks. Her underbelly down there is clean and dry. The engine oil is exactly aligned with the max-mark on the dipstick. It's been a long day, and I don't feel a need to talk to anybody I don't have to. Just to ensure that I don't, I file no flight plan – then fly home visually with no radio contact with anyone.

It is a crystalline, starlit night all the way. No moon. No clouds. Just stars. Number one radio is still *kaput,* but number two is loud and clear if I should need it. I dial it down to barely audible and ease on up to 8500 feet where it's smooth and cool. I then ease the nose around to the dark northwest. At altitude, I ease the power back to lazy, econo-cruise settings. I'm in no hurry. This is the moment I've been waiting for all day. The thin air at this altitude makes it almost quiet. To an outside eye, it might look like solitude. But it isn't. In fact, somehow, it's the opposite. I can feel raw space overflowing all over everything.

Halfway to the stars, I look down on the twinkling lights of hundreds of lives I know absolutely nothing about. The scattered star-dots of heaven above and the sprinkled lights of incandescent civilization below reflect two universes of mirrored sparkle-dust. We glide slowly between them, but part of neither. I turn the instrument lights down to their barest glow. The greatest satisfaction of this moment is that I have the peace of a single observer fresh from an extraordinary lesson in the sacred gulf between the fragility of life and the incredible noisiness of the anxious human spirit. And making it even sweeter, I am in command of an airplane freshly tempered by nature's most brutal aerial anvil.

I have no more words that can describe what I feel right now – other than this is that spiritual moment that all pilots fly for ... and some die for.

Amen.

CHAPTER 3

How to Fly a Deck Chair Home

T HIS PARTICULARLY QUIXOTIC episode in flying experiences unfolds in two phases. The first part is how I came to fly my Mooney down to Bogotá, Colombia. The second is my failed mission to return there a year or so later.

PHASE ONE: Bogatá

Back in the mid-sixties, Juan Manuel Devis was a classmate of mine at Georgia Tech. He and his wife, Carmenza, lived one floor above me in an "affordable" apartment complex in Atlanta. This was one block from the center of the then emerging Hippie District at Tenth & Peachtree Street. Nightlife outside our 2-story compound percolated 24/7. Carmenza was a compelling Latin beauty with gentle brown eyes, a schoolgirl complexion, silken hair and a movie star's smile. She always brought sunshine (and finger food) to the dreariest of those college days. Although all of our apartment building had both running water and flush toilets, it was significantly more modest in size and function than what the newlyweds were accustomed to back home in Bogotá. For me, however, these urban-Atlanta digs were a significant upgrade from my undergraduate years of work-your-way-through-college accommodations up there somewhere in the forlorn snowbelt of mid-Ohio.

Although Juan and I pursued different academic disciplines, I had one big advantage. I could read, write and speak the English language. Not flawlessly, of course. It was more what you might forgivingly call engineer's English. But clearly, Juan held all the other advantages – things like natural grace, a diplomat's poise, humility, humor, incredible intelligence, a rich timber in his voice, a winning smile, and, of course, Carmenza. He could also play the guitar and sing "Coo-ca-<u>roo</u>-ka-coo" whilst rolling the R with long, heartwarming aplomb. On top of that, he was devilishly handsome in that happy, imperially-slim, international manner. You know the type.

For a full school year, we laughed, shared fast-food dinners, partied a little bit, and went together to one whole football game where the Georgia Tech Yellow Jackets lost to the Auburn War Eagles by some score, but who cared? We burned a lot of midnight oil and rode the delightful wave of our most unlikely friendship. Even my high school Spanish got elevated a click or two. *Viva cervezas y camaradería!* See, how's that?

A little over four years after we both graduated and gone our separate ways, I got an unexpected phone call from Juan. He invited me to come down to Bogotá to meet Carmenza's father, Señor Inocencio Ocampo. It seems that Daddy Ocampo needed an architect to design a small office building on a rocky outcropped site in the classy section of town. Two weeks later, on May 17, 1968, I cranked up my old Mooney and headed south.

The most direct air route there is Atlanta - Miami, then across Cuba to Montego Bay, Jamaica. Then there's the big hop over the Caribbean Sea to the port of Barranquilla, Colombia. The last leg is then up across "La Pampa," to the Andes Mountains where Bogotá regally nestles. The total distance is about 2,500 miles. The one-hour flight over *Cuba* was on an airway called Corridor Maya. Upon approaching the island, but still ten miles north of the coastline, I dutifully called Cuba Radio to inform them of my arrival. They didn't respond. I called a second time, this time *en español*. Still no response. Decision time. Either turn around and go back to Key West or keep going until something big happened –something big like getting shot down. I kept going, but without deviating six inches off the centerline of my assigned radio beam. This hour-long leg of the flight turned out to be the longest I have ever held my breath. There was never the first word of response to my dozen calls to their air traffic controllers. When Jamaica finally came up on the horizon, and with no MIGs hot on my tail, I could finally exhale.

This charmingly quiet coastal town is a piece of paradise with plenty of bars, beautiful beaches, street music and sweet ocean breezes. The two days I spent there in tourist-rehab could not have been more welcome.

The extended leg across the Caribbean Sea was long and effortless. After a few experiments in in-flight weight redistribution (as outlined in Chapter 6), the incredible continent of South America came up under my nose. What a feeling that is!

Using my average (at beast) high school Spanish with Approach Control, I landed at the Barranquilla International Airport and checked into a vintage and authentically classic hotel. Everything here in Colombia smelled of history, natural beauty, delicious food, and friendly people. I felt completely comfortable with everyone I met there. But for some reason, I still needed more of this, whatever it is, culture. Two days later, I flew less than an hour west along the Caribbean coastline to Cartagena to check it out. This was purely a tourist visit to see if the town lived up to its melodious name. I needed to confirm that the "g" really is pronounced like an "h." It is.

On my second afternoon there, I was snooping around a closed-off area in the historical fort that guards their harbor against invading pirates. In one of its catacombs, I found a bandaged-up guy standing hidden (or hiding) in one of its unlit cavities. As my eyes gradually adjusted to the blackness of his tomb-like crypt, his image progressively emerged out of the odorous, human-fertilized, underground substrate. My nose found him before my eyes did. We were standing awfully close – perhaps only an arm's length apart. His right arm was taped to his bare chest. When I could finally see his eyes, they were opened wide and he looked afraid. His left hand was behind his back. That was a concern. He did not back up. As you've already guessed, neither one of us was supposed to be there. Without losing what I trusted was eye contact, I slowly nodded and said only, "Señor," and backed away. He stood there motionless, monitoring my retreat. He never uttered a word or sound. As I stepped out of the grotto, painful-daylight-glare never felt so precious.

That night, Juan called me from Bogotá. He politely suggested that I quit poking around in outlying regions and get on with my business mission. Before leaving Cartagena, I inquired at the airport terminal about renting a car to drive this last 500-mile leg. The best information I could gather was that there was no secure highway going across "la pampa". Or maybe they were saying that this was not a safe road for nosey Americanos. I then asked around for an off-road car like a Jeep to rent. Or perhaps a motorcycle to make the trip. I was unable to come up with any such alternate mode of transportation.

Inasmuch as I was already several days behind schedule, I conceded that there really was nothing wrong with taking the easy way to meet my commitment.

How to Fly a Deck Chair Home

It was a pretty day. I cranked up the Mooney, climbed to altitude and headed south to take on the Andes Mountains. Bogotá's big airport, El Dorado International, lies at an elevation of nearly 9000 feet and is surrounded by summits reaching up to 14,000 feet. To clear the afternoon cumuli-buildups and get the best fuel economy, I eased the plane on up to a cruise altitude of 15,000 feet. For the last hour, I went up to 16,000. (The highest I've ever gotten this plane to fly is just shy of 20,000 feet.[2] At that altitude, she wants to either drop her nose to pick up a little speed or slow down and start mushing into a stall. You can still keep her within bounds, but the effort precludes any shade of daydreaming whatsoever. Still, 15,000 feet was high enough to *descend into* El Dorado and not have to weave our way through mountain peaks.

Without an oxygen bottle on board (as required above 12,000 feet), and just to be sure I was keeping all my wits about me, every five minutes, I would write on my kneepad one or two pieces of poetry or prose that I've put to memory over the years. Remember your Rubaiyat? "...Whether your Cup sweet or bitter run, the Wine of Life keeps oozing drop by drop, and the Leaves of Life keep falling one by one."[3]

At 40 miles out, I radioed Bogotá Approach Control. They responded to my Yankee-accented Spanish in crisp, accurate English. They gave headings that kept me far away from the peaks and cleared me down to 11,000 for a visual approach to the runway. The lower altitude brought back that warm, reassuring feeling of blood in my cheeks. It's my experience that you don't miss O_2 until it comes back; then it feels damn-near narcotic. When I was finally lined up on the main runway, I eased back on the

---
[2] The rated service ceiling is 18,800 feet above sea level
[3] https://www.poetseers.org/spiritual-and-devotional-poets/sufi-poets/omar-khayyam/rubaiyat/rubaiyat-verse-5-8/

throttle, pumped down the flaps and lowered the landing gear. As is standard procedure, to help slow the plane down, I pulled the propeller setting to low-pitch and pushed in the fuel-mixture control to full rich just as you're supposed to. The engine then sputtered, stumbled and quit pulling.

The propeller kept windmilling, but it produced no power. I pushed the throttle in for power, but there was no response. Dead engine! Fortunately, the runway was right there under the nose. I still had plenty of altitude to spare, but I also wanted power – *just in case*. An in-flight, engine re-start was a choice, but since I already had plenty of altitude, I concentrated on a perfect "dead stick" landing. Although you're supposed to share little events like the total loss of power with the tower controller, I did not. It doesn't take any engine power to descend, and talking to anybody about it right now seemed more like introducing a distraction that I didn't want to have. My time was much better spent totally focused on a successful landing.

While still a little high on the approach slope (and maybe from lack of oxygen), I dropped the left wing, hit the right rudder, pushed the nose over, and sideslipped the plane to get it down to where I could finally flair for a landing. Everything worked out flawlessly. I greased the wheels on the concrete – no bounce – then slowed to a stop at about the midpoint of the runway. With no airspeed to keep the propeller windmilling, it stopped turning over. So, there I sat, dead center in the middle of El Dorado International with an engine in silent repose. Rather quickly, everything went conspicuously quiet.

The procedure to restart a hot, fuel-injected engine begins with putting the fuel-mixture control in the *off* position. I did this then hit the starter. It fired right up. When I pushed in the fuel mixture control to give it some gas to run on, the engine stumbled and quit again. Ah! I see the problem. I started the procedure over, but this time I eased the mixture control to only *half rich,* and the engine continued to run simply fine. The control tower, probably watching all of this, radioed me to ask what the problem was. I replied that I was just getting organized and asked for directions to taxi to their general aviation facility. Just like I was one of their favorite patrons, they directed me off the runway to a taxiway and then gave me Ground Control radio frequencies.

Ground gave me directions to a cluster of half a dozen private planes over on the far side of the long runway. Once there, I arranged for a tie-down spot, secured the plane, and then from the phone on the service counter, I called Juan Manuel to come pick me up.

Most of the rest of the month in Bogotá was spent setting up an architectural office. Then, with my T-square in one hand and slide rule in the other, I undertook the design of Inocencio's office building. Of course, I had to buy and use a metric scale. At the end of my first morning with Metric, I couldn't believe how medieval inches and feet are. What's wrong with you Gringos up there? Get with it!

The incredible magic of this whole cultural opportunity can be summarized only as one exquisite collection of fragrant and delicious recollections. Some of this wide-eyed *aghast* started with my watching the construction of the 40-story high *bamboo scaffolding* used to construct a skyscraper! This happened right outside the 26th floor window of my small, rented office space. For me, everything in this city was a mild revelation like that. I loved the people, the hustle, the hard work, the music, the fun, the culture, the sophistication, the dangers and the energy. I also discovered, the hard way of course, that anything more than just one courtesy-sip of their *aguardiente* is best left to local professionals.

Yes. I am fully appreciative that I was having the privilege of stepping into the cosmopolitan lifestyle of "the Haves." And everyone knows that the Third World population is more frequently identified with "the Have Nots." But in this case, by a combination of professional circumstances and pure chance, I was exposed to an entirely new view of culture – both rich and poor. Even though my involvement in Bogotá was measured only in weeks, its impact will last a lifetime. Just watch.

PHASE TWO – The Return

It is now December 1969 – a year and a half after my foregoing work-stint in Bogotá. The strong need to go back to see my friends and the fruits of my relationship there has become compelling. But buying an airline ticket simply doesn't have any of what the philosopher John Ruskin called the *Lamp of Sacrifice*. John always wanted to be an architect and wrote an extended essay on it – *The Seven Lamps of Architecture.* He postulated that a lamp is *a light.* And that the Lamp of Sacrifice is one of the lights that adds juice to any effort worth pursuing – (my interpretation). It then follows; the more sacrifice I can add in getting to Bogotá, the happier the spirit of John Ruskin will rest. That certainly makes sense, doesn't it?

Having nothing to do with aviation, a couple of months ago I bought a Yamaha 250cc dual-purpose motorcycle. The idea was to race it in enduros, motocross, trials, cross-country and off-road events. *Dual purpose* means that the machine was both a competition motorcycle and a street-legal ride. It turned out to be barely satisfactory in both endeavors, but it always kicked-started.

The street-legal aspect required the bike to have lights, rearview mirrors and a license plate.

After a 50-mile cross-country race, and while pushing the bike up a ramp and into my van, an idea occurred to me. Suppose I disassemble this thing, put it in the Mooney and flew it down to Barranquilla? I could then reassemble it there and ride it up to and across the Colombian *pampas* to Bogotá – the same pampas I was dissuaded from crossing last year. Then, after reviewing the progress of Inocencio's office building in Bogotá, I would figure out where to go next.

Maybe I'll ride over to the other side of the Andes and down to the Amazon River basin and then over to the town of Leticia. A couple of years ago, I saw a *National Geographic* photograph of a group of aboriginal women gossiping merrily whilst washing clothes waist-deep in the piranha-infested Amazon River. The visual image of these delicate but vulnerable women exposed to the ferocious threat of a piranha attack is hard to dismiss.

Or if that concept doesn't pan out, I could just take the easy option and blaze a new motorcycle path back to Barranquilla. The weather will probably have something to say in how all this will work out. But right now, addressing too many problems too early-on feels a little bit like looking for reasons not to do it. As with nearly all good things in life, when in doubt ... "Ready, fire, aim!"

Obviously, before one gets too committed to any sketchy motorcycle notion, one needs to make a trial-fit to see if the motorcycle can actually fit in the Mooney. Only then can one let notions of fantasy ferment with confidence.

It's a pretty November day at Peachtree Airport, and I'm ready for Step One. I take everything out of the cabin except the pilot's seat. This includes the copilot seat, the back bench seat and the hat shelf in the back. With these removed, I then find that once the wheels and handlebars are taken off the bike, it damn near fits – but not quite. To fully squeeze the bike in, the cabin door needs to come off. The Mooney only has one passenger door and it's on the co-pilot side. After it's removed, the bike snugs in nicely. I then re-hang the door and close it to be sure it closes and latches properly. It does. Then I reopen it and climb over the bike to be sure I can get into the pilot's seat. It's a little gymnastic, but I can. Then I reach over and pull the door closed and latch it. It too works. So much for *proof-of-concept* training.

After removing the bike, it takes about a half a day to get the plane back into normal airworthy mode. Reassembling the motorcycle only takes another couple of hours. The stage is set. It now looks like at least a portion of this next venture can be on two wheels.

Man, am I stoked!

December 14, 1969
Christmas holidays are coming up, and I am heading to Bogotá. Local Flight Service Weather, however, is watching a tropical low-pressure system wend its way westward across Jamaica.

My choice is to either fly through it over Cuba, or go around it. I elect the fair-weather route to go around it by way of New Orleans. From there, I'll go straight across the Gulf of Mexico to Merida, Mexico, and then fly over to San Jose, Costa Rica. Then it's a long, 650-mile leg to Cartagena, Colombia. There, I'll unload and assemble the motorcycle and figure out the best way to get across la pampas to Bogotá. My guess is that the land trip will not be all that difficult. Colombians were traveling all over their country centuries before Mr. Yamaha was born. *Pampas* in English means something like treeless prairie.

I pack two spare motorcycle inner tubes, three extra spark plugs, several headlight bulbs, two quarts of two-stroke oil, a nifty little traveling tool kit, and, most especially, a substantial roll of greenbacks.

Richard Taylor & Nancy Mitchell packing the Mooney.
PDK, Atlanta, December 1968

In a little over 4 hours after leaving PDK, I'm on short final to New Orleans International. The weather forecast for the Gulf of Mexico now includes an even more-generous attendance of thunderstorms. Logic might suggest that I just go find a comfortable motel, let this weather blow through and start fresh in the morning. But there are still too many random energy-cells inside my head that simply will not spool down. Consequently, rather than flying straight through the weather as I had planned, I elect to swing farther west to go around it.

This decision is also in response to the security of the Yamaha. After you've hand-lifted a motorcycle up on a wing, and then gently stuffed it rear-axle first into a small cockpit by yourself, you get the notion that it is forever secure. Also, since there is no practical way to actually lash it down, it ends up just "snugged in." But, once you're airborne and up there closer to heaven, and you compare your incidental weight-lifting efforts to the powerful forces of Mother Nature conducting embedded thunderstorms in your path, your whole perspective of the security of untethered levitation changes. A healthy bump in flight can turn the weight of a 325-pound motorcycle into a lighter than a hot air balloon…until the forces reverse, at which time it weighs more than the plane.

Most of this flight so far has been on instruments in rain and poor visibility, but none of it was in really troubling turbulence. But even normal bumpety-bumps were enough to wave a caution flag. Consequently, I now elect to give any future iffy-weather a wider berth by swinging further west over Central America proper. When I land at Brownsville, Texas, I've been in the pilot's seat for ten hours. This annoying weather system has steadily worked its way over from Cuba. As I said, I ought to slow down and wait it out, but that whatever it is, is still inside my head. I simply have to keep going. As I'm about to fill out my flight plan to Guatemala City, I ask the flight service attendant about the weather along the Pacific coast of Mexico. A more westerly route going south might afford an easier ride around Fidel's tropical, low-pressure folly.

The weather briefer starts with a report for Acapulco. Instead of more meteorological gloom, she offers "clear skies and mild temperatures." This route is hundreds of miles farther west than I need to go, but I've never been there before. Besides, just the sound of *Acapulco* beats the hell out of anywhere else on the map.

This next 700-mile flight takes another four and a half hours. I land there well after dark. It's only a short taxi ride to town where I become the guest of a comfortable, somewhat upscale tourista hotel on that classy crescent-shaped beach that's in all the marketing pictures. This feels so damn good. Finally, I am uncoupled from work-a-day America.

The first thing the next morning, of course, I check the weather report. The fickle, roving meteorological event I've been avoiding has already beaten me to the punch. The skunky stuff that was located southwest of Cuba yesterday has now selected Central America as its next destination of choice.

This image triggers a crazy decision in my head. Rather than filing an instrument flight plan to Guatemala where I will have to take on some real weather turbulence, I pack up my gear and catch a taxi to the airport and walk over to where the Mooney's tied down. The first thing I do is take the door off. By early afternoon, the bike is out of the cockpit and fully assembled for long-distant travel. I fill the gas tank with 100-octane aviation gas and tie-down another plastic gallon jug-a-gas over the taillight bracket. I'm now personally pumped, and the bike is ready to go distances. But sometimes even a guy like me can recognize signs of compulsion. So, just to slow things down a little bit, I re-hang the Mooney door and make myself ride the bike back to my hotel to have a nice dinner, bring this journal up to date, and catch a full night's sleep.

Since the dining room at the hotel is only a quarter full, I pick a table by the window. At dessert, I get into a conversation with two Gringo-suits from California at the next table. They work for an American real estate development company doing a big commercial project here in Acapulco. When I tell them that I am wending my way south to Colombia on my motorcycle, they just look at each other. This is called *a gentleman's scoff*. I don't mention the airplane part of this venture because diversions like that frequently become subjects for discussions other than that which I'd rather talk about.

Then one of them opens the conversation, "Don't even try riding that motorcycle to South America. It's not even possible to drive a car or truck down there. The Pan-American Highway has a sixty-mile gap in it just south of the Panama Canal."

When I ask if a motorcycle could make it through, they say, "No way. There is nothing down there but swamps, jungles, and maybe some mountains. Nothing gets through. If you want to take the Pan-Am Highway to South America, you gotta take a ferryboat around *The Gap*."

The Ismith of Panama

How can a random conversation such as this so quickly ignite the fires of the imagination? These two guys just threw down a gauntlet that, until just now, I had no idea I was looking for. Eventually, they stand up and go off to some social function more worthy of their haughty erudition. As soon as they are out of sight, I gather up the imaginary gauntlet and take it with me back up to my cushy room.

Fortunately, most crazy ideas of this nature die off by dawn's early light. When I wake up this time, however, it is still as alive and vigorous as it was last night. I can't say that I love or hate it, but every time a similar distraction eclipses a larger goal, I'm consciously aware that it *always* comes with a cost. And this is not just a dollar thing. It's time, energy and focus lost on ancillary enthusiasms as well. I won't even discuss broken hearts, bones, promises, commitments and ambitions that get left behind. Almost without exception, pursuing such folly is either *a fool's errand* or an adventure of a lifetime. And too often, the problem is that you never know which way the compass will swing until it's too late to go back and do it the other way.

In any event, the game plan now looks as if I will *ride the motorcycle* down to Bogotá via Guatemala. I have some distant cousins who live in Guatemala City. I've only met the daddy of the family, Col. Oscar Morales y Lopez, a few times, but remember him as a bundle of energy and charisma. He's a five-foot tall, Aztec-looking guy who runs, owns, or flies for a small national airline, Aviateca. I know his son, Sonny, better. Sonny's a handsome and gregarious West Point graduate and, most of all, a pilot's pilot. He and I have something of a distant friendship, but I think he's the kind of guy I can call on for anything – rational or otherwise. Besides, Sonny also flies DC-3s for Aviateca. With either of these Morales cousins, you never quite know where drama ends and reality begins. What more unpredictable opportunity could be so perfect right now?

Once I locate just one of them, for sure they'll show me how to get the motorcycle and me across the Darién Gap to Colombia. Guatemala City is a 750-mile motorcycle ride from here. This is a long haul, but I'm thinking, when I get there, if I go straight to the Guatemala airport, surely somebody there will know, or will know of, the Oscar Morales y Lopez family. Some way or another, I'll figure out how to find them. I'm also thinking that I may have gotten my motorcycle out of the plane way too early. Turbulence or not, I should have flown it to Guatemala City. But that's just hindsight. Right now, my internal go-button is stuck in the *on* position.

After cruising down the highway for more than an hour now, I start to relax.

The endless paved road flows over the horizon in the middle of the great dusty mix of cactus in mid-Mexico. There's not much civilization going on. Every few miles there is some guy either standing or hunkered down along one of the most lonesome stretches of roadbed you can imagine. He might be at an intersection of roads or at a cluster of huts or at some scant sign of agriculture or construction that nobody is working on. He will always be with his machete. He may be waiting for a ride, but I never saw one look like he's asking for anything. Never a thumbs-up. No inquiring gazes. Some of these guys don't even look up. But I also never see one just sitting on his ass, relaxed. He is either standing or hunkered down.

For some reason that I cannot explain (maybe it's boredom), I watch myself shift down a few gears and stop to offer one of these guys a ride. Like the others I've seen, this guy is mostly nondescript: average height, dark face with deep-sculpted wrinkles, dressed like everybody else out here with dark brown or gray baggy clothes. Zooming by at 60 miles per hour, you can't tell any of their ages. But when you slow down, you sure do take notice of one thing – how big that machete is. I mean, these things are dragon-slaying weapons – fierce enough to have a personal name like *El Conquistador* or *El Equilizitoro*. As I gesture to my prospective passenger to climb aboard, I have something of a flash-thought about the wisdom of my decision. With neither conversation nor hesitation, the guy straddles the back half of the motorcycle saddle-seat. He positions himself threateningly close to me. To hold on, he puts his left arm firmly around my stomach like I'm already his captive. "El Equilizitoro" is in his right hand. I snick the bike into first gear, ease out the clutch and down the road we accelerate. Once we're at 60 mph, I'm safe. Holding cruise speed gives me a little time to wonder what the hell I was thinking by picking up this guy.

Thirty miles later, as we're approaching an intersecting dirt road that has no visible enterprise, *mi amigo*, in a grumbly voice, hollers something unintelligible in my ear. It sounds like, "I'm going to cut you up into little bitty pieces and make Gringo Taco out of you." I slow down and stop. He dismounts with a deadpan expression and says, "Macho gracias," and starts walking down the intersecting dirt road that looks like it goes to another Nowhere. Cautiously, I shift slowly through the gears and ease on south. For some reason, I clearly do not want *mi amigo* to know how relieved I am.

Just as the sun is setting, I enjoy a most welcome *pollo con arroz* dinner in a six-rooms-in-a-row motel that is still under construction. The roof, all the walls, and the floors are erected; it's dried-in, but not finished. A few rooms are furnished with already well-worn beds and dressers. The unfinished cantina at the end of the row is operational but can accommodate only three or four guests. Only one bathroom in this small complex is operational. The owner and his wife are gracious almost to the extreme. They tell me that I'm their first *motocicleta* guest.

The door to my room has no lock, but it does have a doorknob. The door swings out. I find a four-foot piece of two-by-four to span the opening, and I did bring a tow rope. The Yamaha slept standing up in the corner of the room.

The next morning, I'm on the road at sunup and my program finally seems to be taking on some sense of order. The Pan-American Highway runs north–southish along the western lower third of Mexico. As this main-artery highway journeys south, it eases inland through Guatemala City. From there, it runs farther south through the countries of El Salvador, Nicaragua, Costa Rico and then to Panama. From there, I'll figure out how to snake my way through the Darién Gap to Colombia. But right now, rather than continuing this hasty, albeit boring, route south, I decide to follow a secondary road to the west of the Pan Am Highway. This secondary road runs parallel to the Pacific coast. Traveling these more coastal roads may also offer some off-road experiences that might be helpful at The Gap. In any event, it will be better than this awfully long and thoroughly uneventful highway routine at only one featureless mile per minute.

In southern Mexico, the Pan-American Highway is the closest parallel main highway to the ocean. But in many, if not most places, it runs 10 or 20 miles inland from the ocean. Then intermittent, sometimes unpaved umbilical's lead from this great highway west through the jungle to resort townships or indigenous villages with an ocean view.

After exploring several of these ins and outs to dead ends, I arrive at a modestly scaled village whose name I cannot determine. I say *village*, but it has neither paved roads nor visible commerce. It is not inhospitable in any way, but it offers no resorts or hospitality facilities that I can find. Along the broad, sandy beach where it meets the jungle are four or five thatched roof huts roughly aligned with the edge of the jungle's vegetation border. The living level in the huts is elevated eight feet or so above grade. The ground level is undecked and unpaved and serves as a shelter for a collection of what looks like "just family junk." All the structures face the ocean but gain some weather protection from the dense foliage of the trees and vegetation in which they nestle. The small building-cluster I'm looking at now is at the intersection of a hundred-foot-wide fresh-water river/stream that flows gently out of the jungle and perpendicularly into the ocean. Curiously, there is no delta formation – just a wet tee-intersection. I haven't been checking the moon lately, but maybe it's a tide thing.

On the river and about at the tree line of the houses, there are three or four small, open boats moored to a simple wooden dock. As a teenager, I worked for my uncle, Captain Lerch Crandell, on the Chesapeake Bay in Shady Side, Maryland. He was a second-or third-generation waterman whose primary livelihood was oystering. In the oyster off-season (months without an R), he and I netted small bay shrimp that he sold to a local tackle store who resold them as bait. If this job sounds menial, it did not seem so at the time. Not even a little bit. Making a living off nature's generosity is a life experience on many levels. Right now, the gravitational pull from these fisherman's workboats in this far corner of Mexico feels natural. I have little choice but to yield to instincts.

I park the motorcycle under a tree and walk over to a guy with a big-billed fisherman's cap. He's wearing a bleached-out blue shirt and working at the foot of a palm tree on what looks like crab or lobster pots. In my best improvised *español*, I ask him if he needs some help. He only half smiles and says, "No. Gracias, Señor." I tell him that I have another question and ask about how best to get my motorcycle and me across this little river so I can negotiate farther south along the coast. He's politely patient and asks my destination. I say, "Guatemala."

Incidentally, the guy looks like he might be the brother of yesterday's highway passenger. He has that same waterman's speech-cadence as Uncle Lerch, i.e., he thinks before he says anything. Because of my language limitations, the conversation is something of a struggle. We both speak slowly. What I understand he is saying is that for the next 50 kilometers or so, the forest and jungle come right down to the ocean as it does here. He says that my motorcycle cannot get through. Then he points out the obvious: that even though there is not a bridge right here, this condition of not being able to cross the tributary rivers will be repeated in each of the villages for the next 50 kilometers farther south. His argument suggests that I need to backtrack and take the big, boring, paved Pan-American Highway to Guatemala. Since this is what I *do not* want to hear, I ask him, "Señor, es posible que usted ... take me and my motorcycle in *your* boat the next fifty kilometers south?"

In the back of my mind, this proposal mimics what I might have to do at the Darién Gap. Sure, putting the bike on a boat is a compromise I'm not anxious to make, but I've also been giving some thought to super-inflating the two spare inner tubes I brought with me to float across and these small waterways, *and maybe the Gap*. But where we are now is way too civilized to get into that mode of thinking.

Besides, if I'm ever going to get to Bogotá, I've got to keep pressing on.

Before answering my question about his taking the bike and me in his boat, he looks over his shoulder at the village back along the tree line. To me this means he's giving my proposal consideration. Then he looks back at me and answers, "No, friend. My boat is for fishing. It is too small for you, me, *y motocicleta*."

But I think I caught a slightly too-long hesitation before he answered. It makes me think he might really want to do this thing, but he's probably struggling with practicality. Right off, I feel like I'm the perfect guy to help him with this. So, I ask him if he will show me his boat. We walk over to one of those moored at the dock. Technically, his is not a dugout canoe. It's a heavy-hulled open boat formed by several large logs planed down to heavy, curved planks that are then secured together with lag bolts and wooden dowel-fittings to only a few, very oversized ribs. The bow is pointy in the traditional manner, and there is an old, paint-faded Evinrude outboard motor secured to the three-inch thick blunt transom. The length of the boat is about eighteen feet, with a beam of a little over three feet. It's heavy and stout. But even empty, it doesn't have much freeboard between the waterline and the gunwales. Obviously, this is a river workboat, not an open-water, ocean-going vessel. Without question, she makes her living working upstream from here. The biggest issue with taking her out to sea, as I see it, will be weather conditions relevant to wave action and surface chop.

Mi amigo and I don't discuss center-of-gravity (CG) issues. But I do suggest that we might lie the bike on its side and place it about midship. His intuitive sense of the physics concerning CG doesn't need my book-informed contribution. I know that. As I stumble with my Español, I watch his eyes. I just want him to know that I haven't accepted his decline to motor the three of us down the coast.

Obviously, it's now time to switch the conversation from naval-physics to economics. In the form of a question, I propose a $50 fare. His understanding of this subject requires only the time it takes for him to raise his eyebrows and look *me in the eye* to see if I'm serious. I nod and smile the faintest tad I can muster. He raises his eyebrows an equal tad and we make the deal right then and there. No bickering. No bartering. Hence forth, el nombre de mi amigo es *El Capitán*. Yo soy, *Señor Ricardo*.

15 of the 16 Dumbest Things I Have Ever Done in an Airplane

El Capitán does not go home to check with Señora Capitán or pick up food or extra fuel. He simply helps me wrestle the Yamaha over onto its side, and we rope it securely onto his boat. It hangs generously over both gunwales. The throttle is in the water. I sit between the bike and the bow. It takes El Capitán ten hefty pulls to get the old Evinrude to finally fire up, and we then smoke our way out of the river and onto the boundless expanse of the mighty Pacific Ocean.

The sea is not calm. For me, it stays right on the edge of *don't go*. Of course, there are no life jackets on board. I have my Swiss Army knife in my pocket, closed but at the ready to cut the motorcycle tie-downs should we swamp and need to dump the bike quickly. I look back at the two mounting points of the Evinrude. If dumping the bike isn't enough to keep the boat afloat, then I'll unscrew the engine clamps by hand to drop the motor. This won't take but a few seconds. Without these two heavy objects, even swamped, the heavy-planked boat should be buoyant enough for the two of us to hold on to. Maybe, we'll even be able to bail it out to serve as our lifeboat. There is only one oar on board. So, if we do have to dump the motor, we should be able to skull ourselves to shore. El Capitán seems comfortable with my not sharing any of my safety plans with him.

We putt-putt along nicely at what I guess to be almost a jogging pace – maybe 9 or 10 knots. There is no real sea running, but it's still a wet ride through a slapping-chop. Having only one large soup can, El Capitán and I alternate bailing. This is a continuous but not at all unpleasant duty. Since we may be bailing only bow-spray, I cannot tell whether the hull leaks or not. We're both wet, but it's a beautiful day and we're just two guys with lifted spirits – each in our own way, enjoying the innocent narcotic of small adventure.

Five hours at sea is not a long time, but we did have to refuel from his backup metal jug. But I gotta tell you, the wind has been picking up, and when we finally pull into the dock at our destination village, I'm plenty ready for this phase to be overwith.

We moor at a dock located on the *south* side of a river intersecting with the ocean. I have no idea where we are now, but the quietude is a graciously welcomed relief from the endless ocean and the noise of that faithful Evinrude. Along with a very firm handshake, I pay my fare to El Capitán with 5 greenback tens. For only the second time today, he smiles. This time, he abbreviates the farewell expression with only "Con Dios, amigo." I watch him walk over to talk to a couple of guys at the gas pump. They look like old friends. Then, in unison, all three look over my way. He then goes back in his boat, pulls the Evinrude starter cord a dozen times, casts off and still at a leisurely pace, smokes his way back north. Without question, he now has a good Gringo story to share with Señora Capitán and the kids.

What I liked most about this little chance encounter was that my captain's thinking was a little ahead of mine. I'm too used to thinking that all rivers at civilized points have bridges. El Capitán's brain was making a trip that I couldn't see. He understood where I needed to end up – that is, at a village on the *south* side of an intersecting river. This way, I would be able to continue worming my way farther south for at least one more river intersection. Still, for some reason, my trust in the man makes me proud. Maybe it's just the *mano a mano* thing. Again, I don't know what it is. It just is. And it's damned good. And that's enough said about it.

Now here I sit, back on my scooter. It's a beautiful afternoon. There is about a hundred miles of gas in the tank. I'm no longer the least bit worried about being swamped by a rogue wave. I also have not eaten today, but I have money in my pocket. I don't know where I am or even where I'm going next. I can think of no liberation on the face of the earth that can offer a traveler more satisfaction than where I am right now.

Apparently, however, I'm not quite ready for all the wind-in-the-face thing, so I dismount and walk over to an open-air cantina. Even when you enjoy being a little hungry, food still helps to get you back to the here and now. The meal turns out to be the obligatory chicken chunks and rice. And that's fine. I eat it slowly just to postpone having to make any decisions about where to go next.

The *pollo* charges my battery, and I end up cranking the bike and just snaking my way down the coastline heading southeast. The next bite-sized civilization is a township called *Puerto Escondido* (Hidden Port). This place feels more like a local *Mexicana* resort than a *Gringo*-tourist destination.

Today is Christmas Eve. I check in at a tidy but modest two-story hotel a block from the beach. It's quiet here. The desk clerk, Miguel, speaks easy-English and directs me to two points of interest in town – their beach and their big church (not quite a small cathedral). A thought flashes through my mind. Maybe I could just put my feet up here and *coast on the Coast* for a week. But that's crazy thinking. I need to stay focused. Puerto Escondido is still a magical little town where prowling around in the old village architecture and snooping the natural ocean caves up the coast is fully rewarding.

On the other hand, as one might expect, Christmas Eve, even with a tropical sunset, can still be a little bit lonely. Walking around town after dinner, I heard a couple of carols en Español.

On Christmas morning, I'm ready to start making miles. The Yamaha kicks right to life, and we head inland and up to the romantic mountain town of Oaxaca.

I hate like hell to give up on my ambition to blaze a new Gold Coast Route to Panama – and then to *The Gap*. But right now, my job is to keep all those wonderful (but annoying) notions at bay. I need to get to the big action – Bogotá.

One hour into the new day's adventure, and wouldn't you know it? The next unscripted event in this journal unfolds.

I'm cruising along at my easy 60 on an improved (gravel) roadbed that runs through terrain that looks like a once-vegetated but now-dehydrated and scorched wasteland. Since I wear eyeglasses to correct astigmatism, I don't wear goggles. There is no helmet law in Mexico, consequently, highway cruising is all about air-in-the-hair.

Then, whop! An insect, or something of substance, hits the rim of my glasses and plants its corpse or guts (or poop) in the outside corner of my right eye. I never see it, but the impact, or my reaction to it, twitches my head back. This is no wimpy fruit-fly. It has mass. I slow down briskly and pull over to the rocky drainage ditch along the edge of the road to scrape the yuck out. There is too much of it to just wipe off by hand. With the bike on its kickstand and canteen in hand, I swab out as much goo as I can. Wipe as I might, there remains residual stinging that won't wipe away. Even after fifteen minutes of mopping and swabbing, it's still gooey. I huddle up to the little, round rearview mirror on the handlebars to see what's going on. But I can't really distinguish my eye-juices from foreign ingredients.

After thirty minutes of just sitting here, my eyeball is still scorching hot. The eyelid from eye brow to eye lashes is now puffing out and looks pretty disgusting in the little mirror. No vehicle has driven by in either direction since I've been here. I have to admit it that I'm starting to worry a bit.

I'm out here in Ninguna Parte[4], Mexico and have no idea where the closest hospital is. Oaxaca, a big dot on the road map,

---
[4] Nowhere

is about 60 miles in the mountains up ahead. Call it an hour ride. I'm sure that they will have adequate medical facilities there. I have made several trips to Mexican hospitals in the past. Every time, I felt the doctors were experienced and competent. But I also sensed that their facilities never had enough of that comforting pomp and circumstance and glittering equipment with lots of dials, lights and gauges we have back home.

Puerto Escondido is an hour behind me. Yesterday, by chance, I walked past their full-sized clinic. My guess is that I'm currently about 350 miles from Acapulco and the Mooney. Call that five hours away. If my eye gets any worse, one way or another, I'll eventually need to get back to my airplane.

Right now, I'm just sitting here. The eye has now swollen itself completely shut. I just squeezed it from the two sides to see if I can make it open enough to let the juices out, but it won't quite do it. It just stays dark, wet, and burning inside.

I'm not confident about what the best course of action is right now. But I do know one thing for sure. Fiddling around out here on my butt with an eyeball that's maybe filled with acid-etching condor poop, ain't getting it. I kick-start the bike, swing it around, and head back to Puerto Escondido. This way, if things get worse, at least I'll be closer to my plane.

After an hour's ride, I go straight to my old hotel. Miguel is somebody I feel I can trust and fortunately he's working the front desk. But before I check in, I explain (and show) him my problem. He completely shares my urgency to do something and suggests using the city clinic.

But before we get into any immediate medical planning, in a rare moment of rationality, I abandon my normal stubborn independence and ask his help to place a long-distance call to Nancy Mitchell and Associates in Atlanta. Nancy and I have been dating pretty steadily for a couple of years. Other than being just another beautiful woman, she is resolutely independent and has one of the most highly respected interior design firms in town. She is also a licensed pilot. After nearly fifteen minutes on hold, I get her on the phone.

"Mitch, I haven't gotten to Colombia yet. I'm down here in Mexico somewhere and have an eye problem. The Mooney is back at the Acapulco airport. How about catching a flight and meeting me there this evening. Then if you will fly me back to Atlanta tomorrow, and I'll get it all fixed up."

There is a pause. She then asks, "Can you see out of the eye?"

"Well, no. It's swollen shut. But I can see out of the other one."

"Why don't you just go to a hospital and get it looked at?"

Even though I knew she was going to ask that, I still don't have any particularly good answer. "Well, I'm going to. I just haven't found the right one yet."

She takes a little time to think, then says, "I'm sorry, but I cannot leave right now. But if you can't find a hospital, why don't you just go see a regular doctor? It may be just a bug bite. And then if you still need some help, I'll check on flights for tomorrow afternoon. But right now, why don't you just go get a doctor to look at it." Sometimes, even very bright people's thinking patterns are so damned predictable.

Simultaneously, I'm thinking about the several hundred-mile motorcycle ride to Acapulco. If I *left-eye* up there right now, I should be able to get my bad-eye checked at their hospital this evening. They'll probably just put goo and salve all over it and maybe bandage it up. I'm also thinking maybe Nancy can then turn up tomorrow evening to fly me and my gooey eyeball back home.

One thing I know for sure – whether it's lineal thinking or not – I need to get closer to my airplane. I answer Mitch, "Sure. Catch as early a flight as you can. Send me the bill, okay?" I did mention that she's a businesswoman, didn't I?

I do not check into the Puerto Escondido hotel. Miguel just looks at me as I shake his hand, say thanks and go back out their front door and kick-start the motorcycle and snick it into gear. I need to get going. A bandage over my swollen eye might look better, but it wouldn't do anything. It's already sealed-shut tight as a tick. I put on my prescription sunglasses and wick on the throttle.

Riding a motorcycle with one eye takes a little more getting used to than you might think. But, if there's no choice, it's doable.

It's sunset, when I get to Acapulco. The swelling pressure has lessened. I can now manually spread the eye open to a peep-slit and see out. That first glimmer of light is hugely encouraging. I assume it means that the eyeball is still operational. With sunglasses hiding my disfiguration, I check back into my fancy tourist hotel and order a room-service dinner. I also leave a message with my new contact info on Nancy's office answering machine in Atlanta.

In the morning, the eye is still swollen but not nearly as much as it was yesterday afternoon. Because I still look so grotesque, today I decide to just sit out on the beach with my sunglasses on to see if it's going to do any more healing on its own. I hesitate to admit this, but I also rinse my eye out with ocean water and then let it dry in the sun. Yes. I know. This is an old witch's brew, but when I worked for Uncle Lerch on the Chesapeake, bay-water (which is only brackish) used to cure cuts and scrapes pretty nicely.

The next morning, Nancy calls around 10:00 a.m. She's booked a flight and will arrive here tomorrow late morning. Man, what a wave of relief. I go back in the beach and ocean-flush the eye some more. I even open my eye under the water and spread the eyelids so the brine can get everywhere. I can only hope that the municipal sewerage treatment plant isn't too close. By midafternoon, the swelling is three-quarters gone. It has now progressed from being patently grotesque to just ordinary-ugly.

The next day, when I pick Nancy up at the airport, there is only scant evidence of there ever having been any eye problem at all. I never did go to either a doctor or a hospital. This curious tale takes some serious explaining to the freshly arrived Florence Aviatrixingale. Thank goodness the white part of the eyeball is still bloodshot-red. In the end, I believe she really does buy the entire bug-in-the-eye story.

So here we are, stranded in Acapulco with a motorcycle full of gas, money still in my pocket, two good eyes, and absolutely nothing to do but entertain Mitch.

It is with no small sense of pride that I parade her around town on the back of the Yamaha with a Peach State license plate. I believe that showing her off to the rest of the working-class gawkers, and lazy idle-rich, helps the curing process even more than the ocean-flush. And, since you didn't ask, no, she doesn't hold on nearly as tight as my friend with El Equilizitoro. She rides as you are supposed to – balancing so in sync with the bike that you hardly know anyone's back there.

We spend a couple of days exploring the area and relaxing in one of the loveliest havens in the developed world. Having had about all the adventure I could stand; I drop the motorcycle off at a Yamaha dealership and have it crated and shipped to Atlanta. Two of us can now travel in my plane.

While checking out at the hotel front desk, for five dollars, I buy one of their folding deck chairs. This will be used as a copilot seat. After loading our personal gear in the plane, the new PIC sits in the cushiony left seat, and I jimmy into the deck chair where the motorcycle was, but sans seatbelt. I have no clue why this feels so just-right, but somehow it does.

In the four years following this event, Nancy's interior design firm will expand in scale and grow in recognition. My architectural partnership will also flourish. We will marry and raise three children: Nancy Lee, Ruthie, and RT-III. They, in time, will present us with five perfect grandkids – Evan, Gordon, Richard Owen, Hadley, and RT-IV. Later on, Lee adds Libby and Ben. Naturally enough, until this book is finished, none of these seven youngsters will have a clue about how all this family stuff suffered incubation.

And the Darién Gap is still there. I gave it a go and didn't even get there. But as you see, just challenging something almost unreachable can change a life forever.

Now it's your turn. Good luck my friend. I hope you do as well as I.

CHAPTER 4

'Tis a Fool's Errand That Seeks a Bridge Too Far

T HE FIRST TIME I heard the *Fool's Errand* idiom, I had to Google it to confirm its meaning. The most colorful example I found was "a glass hammer driving glass nails." In other words, *a fool's errand* enjoys a fairly predictable outcome – and it's usually much less than you expected. Please keep this admonition in mind as I offer here a living example of its execution.

It all started with my brother, Owen, calling me in Atlanta from his home in Annapolis. In his carefully measured lawyer-turned-fundamentalist-preacher's voice, he told me that our father was in the hospital there. Apparently, he's recently been in and out of treatment for chronic bladder cancer issues. Since Dad had never shared any of his personal health issues with me, I haven't given it much thought. The real truth of the matter is, our father-son relationship was never the comfort blanket that either one of us wanted it to be. It's that weather-worn song we've all heard about high expectations and low deliverable goods.

Fundamentally, he always wanted his first son to *be something* – maybe an esteemed scholar or a respected business guy, or, at the very least, a successful (well-to-do) anything. My personal ambitions, however, were less aspiring. I just wanted to *do things*. Things like build Soap Box Derby racers, or remote-control model airplanes, or maybe even a hydroplane-speedboat. And when I did those things, they were just tinkerer's achievements that were seldom recognized on anybody's social calendar – nor, more importantly, on any schoolteacher's grade sheet. To make things worse, even modest scholastic achievement was not in my wheelhouse. With only a few exceptions did Dad's and my mutual expectations ever align.

But, as everyone knows, there are always two perspectives to every personal skirmish. Dad's ambitions, naturally were based on his life-experience. His was a story of being raised in a parentless, tenement-house situation in Hell's Kitchen, and then working his way up to the suburban, middle-class comfort of Chevy Chase, Maryland. This involved his switching roles from being a gas pump jockey to an ambitious shirt-and-tie, real estate juggler. It was a huge step, but he measured up to it. He and Mom then had three children, two of whom excelled in just about anything they undertook. I was the middle kid with a learning curve flat enough to shoot a game of marbles on.

Yes, I know. This is about as time-worn a theme as a conspicuous-underachiever story gets. But in my own defense, all this happened before attention-deficits became the excuse of choice for just about any academic underperformance. The same goes for dyslexia. In other words, back then there was precious little patience for what was generously viewed upon as *a Lazy*

Brain. In those days the solution to the LB problem was really quite simple – just tighten-up on the discipline screws.

In my senior year in high school, the screw-tension exceeded what I considered to be my tolerance level. In November, 1953, at eighteen years old, I packed a grocery bag of my clothes and left home. And, yes, a month later, after dark, I did sneak back to their house to peek in the windows to see the Christmas tree all lit up and happy. A couple of years after that, my job of pumping gas at 25 cents per hour wasn't meeting my needs. This led me to a US Army Recruiting Office. Unless you've been there, you would never believe how empowering is to have underwear again. Believe it or not, for some of us, it's way up there with luxuries like eating 3 meals a day. So, I signed up.

After basic infantry training, I was sent to my first school of higher learning, the 82nd Airborne Jump School.

Incredibly modest though it was, earning paratrooper wings and wearing spit-shined jump-boots and a form-tailored uniform was my first introduction to the empowering notion of *personal achievement.*

Three years later, now as a Korean War Vet, I undertook civilian life as a day laborer at construction sites. I still liked the idea of building things, but learned rather quickly that pick-and-shovel work was too much like my former life as an infantry grunt. I then secured a job at the Addressograph-Multilith Company. They saw a little something in me and sent me to their factory in Cleveland, Ohio to learn about repairing office copiers.

The fattish, busy-body old lady who ran the boarding house I lived in liked me enough to gave me milk and homemade cookies if I would read the books she lent me. One of the books was *The Fountainhead* by Ayn Rand. The hero of the book, an architect named Howard Roark, was not an elite academician. He liked to design and construct things. He was also a guy who took little notice of the traditional obstacles in life. Without distraction, he just followed his own visions and ambitions. As improbable as it sounds, my goal in life then became being an *architect* just like him. Now how completely unlikely and selfish is that?[5] I think Ms. Rand would approve.

However, there was a glitch here. To be an architect requires a college degree. When I told my boarding house lady about this, she said she thought I could do it. And when she said it, she didn't blink. Still, for me to undertake this academic-impossibility, I needed to double-bait the hook. And most importantly, for me at least, the other challenge needed to be achievable.

So, I made an oath that I shared with no one – not even the boarding house lady: *If I ever finish college, I will reward myself by getting a license to fly an airplane – a real one –and one I don't have to "un-ass"*[6] *unless I want to.*

Besides, I knew I could fly. I did it every day in my head.

The GI Bill provided tuition, and I was accepted (on probation) as an in-state student in a no-nonsense college, Kent State University. Almost immediately, they taught me how to book-learn. It turned out to be unexpectedly simple. Dumb kids simply have to work twice as hard as bright kids. Well, hell, I thought. Anybody can do that. Even me!

In retrospect, the innocence of my ignorance was both a problem and a strength. For instance, I was well into my freshman year before I discovered that the bachelor's degree program in Architecture, was not a four-year course. *It was five-year course!* This added year was followed by a three-year internship of drafting servitude before one was eligible to take a one-week-long

---

[5] Rand also wrote, "The Virtue of Selfishness" – an incredible read
[6] Airborne Jump Master jargon for "Jump." For instance: "When I slap the number-one guy in *the jump stick* to unass this bird, he better already have one foot on the threshold and his hands on the jambs!"

test for professional licensure (one that fewer than half of the applicant's passed the first time). None of that was mentioned in *The Fountainhead*. But remember. My boarding-house lady said that I could do it. And, quite innocently, I trusted her.

To make ends meet, concurrent with full time school, I worked as a draftsman for a residential builder in nearby Hudson, Ohio. Incrementally, my grades improved to *full tuition forgiveness* levels. In fact, they got to where Graduate School at Georgia Tech was on a "full-boat" scholarship; *I didn't even need an outside job!*

A year after graduation, I passed my Architectural Registration Exam and started my own professional practice.

But I gotta be honest. Absolutely *none* of this quick bio went nearly as smoothly as I just made it sound. Not even close. If I were to retell it filling in all the cracks, it would be cobbly, circuitous, frustrating, unlikely, out of plumb, and full of stupid mistakes, disappointments and wrong turns. And most of all, it was about as un-fun as struggling ambition gets. In any event, however, no matter in what key this story is played, at least you now know everything worth knowing about me, and I still have absolutely no idea about you sitting there reading all this, and wondering, "where the hell is this guy going with all this off-the-wall, biographical blather?"

Well, in architectural vernacular, it's called Foundation Work. But in a pilot's lounge it might just be called **B**lowing **S**moke.

Either way, back to the story:

After my brother's phone call yesterday about our father being in the hospital, I got to thinking. The weather all along the entire East Coast of America is flat-ass beautiful. I'm almost caught up at work in the office, so what the heck. *If Dad is in the hospital, maybe I will just pay the old goat a surprise visit. Now that would be a hoot. I haven't talked to him in months.*

Any proactive act of kindness on my part toward him would be something I've never given much consideration to. Even if I just turn up at the hospital, I have no idea what he will think, or what his reaction might be.

More importantly – to me, at least – I have no idea about what *I* will feel. Subconsciously, I wonder if I might be going there just to gloat over his debilitation. This is not a reaction one takes much pride in.

Still, with an annoying sense of uncertainty, I drive straight out to Peachtree Airport and make a call to my business partner, Jim Williams, to tell him where I'm going.

Visiting my father is still an open option. But if I want to change my mind at any time, I can just land at the Annapolis airport, rent a car and drive over to the commercial docks in the downtown historical district right between the US Naval Academy and the State Capitol. There on the dock I'll enjoy two juicy soft-shell crab sandwiches, an order of fries, and an over-sized lemonade to wash it all down. There is something almost alluring about a fresh, soft-shell meal right in the middle of the brackish, diesel smell of the harbor. However, this plays out, I will have plenty of this beautiful morning *alone* at altitude to sort out any minor technicalities.

Three and a half soul-soothing hours later, I turn left base leg in the landing pattern, pump down full flaps and lower the landing gear to line up on the narrow airstrip at Lee Airport. On final approach, I can still see both the tiered dome of the State Capitol and the Naval Academy complex just a few miles to the north. Just beyond it are the graceful, inverted catenary cables of the Chesapeake Bay Bridge.

The fellow running the desk at the airport's small terminal building is an agreeable sort and accepts my business proposal, i.e., if I fill up my airplane with his gas, he'll lend me his car to go into town for a couple of hours. We both smile, shake hands on it and I'm headed to town.

With detached amazement, I then watch myself drive straight to the hospital. *What the hell is going on? I thought I was up here for a crab feast on the dock of the Bay. Who's in charge here, anyway?*

The good part about the way this is all playing out, however, is how comfortable I am in slipping into the observer's role.

In the hospital lobby, the receptionist tells me that a Richard Taylor, Sr., is in room 229. I take the elevator up to the second floor of this comfy, Marriot-feeling facility. There is not even a hint of Lysol, or whatever it is that hospitals use to make them smell like a hospital.

Door 229 is ajar, but I knock anyway. There is no response. I feel more nervous than I want, but I push the door the rest of the way open. The room is darkish. The TV is not on but there is someone sitting up in the bed. He looks up at me but seems neither surprised nor pleased. But he is also not displeased. I'm thinking, *I bet he feels like me right now –something like an observer.*

This is the first time in my life that I have ever seen him not-in-control of everything around him – including me – maybe, especially me. I am looking at a frail old man. I walk over to the head of his bed and put my hand on his shoulder. It's all knobby bones. It used to be smooth and solid like a polished granite statue. I stand here, healthy, strong and clearly in control of the situation. But this is not where I want to be. I want to be inside *my* full armored suit – in my old defensive stance with one foot forward and the other back to absorb the impact. I want to be the cautious, semi-closed person who is prepared for either thrusts or parries. I want to play my old defense-game. En garde!

But there is no game going on. We are simply looking at each other through personal vacuums.

"Hello, Dad."

He says, "Hello, son."

"You doin' all right?"

"Yes. I'm all right."

"I came to see you."

"I can see that."

Man, this isn't working at all. To regroup a little, I walk away from his bed and over to the plate-glass window on the south facing wall. As I look back at him over on the darker side, he's frail and hollow-eyed in his half-raised hospital bed. His nightshirt is falling off his old man's narrow shoulders. The acetylene blue in his eyes is faded to a flat gray. There is no light coming out. His rugged complexion is as white as his bedsheet. He needs a shave. His thin, white hair is frazzled and unkempt. For a second, from across the room, I catch just a notion of his male scent. Like a snap of a whip, it makes me twitch. But that smell is impossible, so I try to erase it. Maybe I just imagined it anyway.

The wide window next to me looks south over a tributary creek. Along its bank are several small fiberglass pleasure boats neatly berthed in their slips. They look like properly stored toys. At midstream, there is a kid trying to sail an 8-foot skiff, but there is no wind. The whole landscape is an antiseptic movie set – elegant but unreal. So unreal that my mind drifts right out of the room we're in. It's in search of something easy to light on. *That kid needs to learn to* scull *his boat.* Even with that blink of a thought, I feel guilt. The old man right behind me taught me how to scull (propel a boat with a single oar in a notch in the transom) before I was big enough to keep two oars in their locks. What a precious, corn-ball memory. Surely, I don't need that kind of annoying business in my head right now. I move back to

'Tis a Fool's Errand That Seeks a Bridge Too Far

the foot of the bed so I can test that smell-event again. For some crazy reason, this scent detection notion is the only substantive idea formulating in my mind right now.

Since I can think of nothing constructive to talk about, I ask, "How do you feel about dying? Are you ready to go?" As soon as I hear these biting words, I wonder why in the name of hell I just posed such an incredibly painful question. I didn't hold his hand or call him "Dad." I didn't even look into his frosty eyes. That insensitive question was so inexcusable on so many levels. But there it was. I was so stunned and ashamed that I couldn't think of any way to talk it back. I just stood there, dumbfounded at my unsympathetic tactlessness.

His answer comes out slowly from somewhere deep inside – rather like he expected it. "No. I don't want to die." There was no hint of self-pity in this response nor any shock at the insensitivity of my asking it.

As I look at him, I don't quite understand why he just let me off the hook. The Category 5 father who blew down everything in his path – including me – is looking across the length of his hospital bed vacantly, saying he doesn't want to die. I cannot grasp any of this.

There is another period of silence, and I mentally ask myself, "Well, do *I* want him to die?"

Of course, I don't know the answer to this. But I think it's *no*. I want him to spool up, to start knocking things down again. I want the perfect storm to re-erupt and mete out every kind of pain, anguish, guilt, and uncertainty that makes life … *life*. I want him to look through me with those cutting-torch eyes and make me stand up to whatever miserable failure he thinks I am. Even as I move back into the direct sunlight from the window, for some reason, I feel I am so not here; that I can no longer even cast a shadow in this patient room. Maybe *I'm not* here. For the first

81

time in my life, I have turned into the aggressor with this man. This is not at all the way this morning was supposed to play out.

It is only now that I ask myself why I came here to the hospital, mano a mano. Was it to finally establish territory?

Well, let me tell you this. You can't self-evaluate in the presence of a whispering ghost. There is absolutely no territory in any part of this equation.

The fragile frame I am looking at simply disarms the power-offence I didn't know I brought with me into this room. This hits me so hard I want to sit down. Of course, I don't. I can't. Sitting would be capitulation. It might make me be something I'm not. It might even suggest that I want to lay down my sword. This incredibly cruel idea of my seeking unwanted dominance over a dying man – my father – hollows my stomach with guilt. I get lightheaded, but I'll die dead on this floor before I sit down.

Then, another thought runs through my mind: Forget dominance. *Maybe I'm standing here still begging for my father's approval?*

This concept hurts too. But I think I'm not buying it. I think that part of our relationship ended with my first step into this room. Besides, the old man here in this hospital room is not my father. This is not the man I would stand up to, toe-to-toe and always lose. *My* father is not in this room.

I have no idea what this attitude says about me as a son – or a man. But we all know damn good and well, it can't be good. My only virtue right now, is that I am drenched to the core in hot, molten guilt – or something so similar to it that it hurts just as much. Maybe it's whatever I think I am, or hope I am, but I'm not.

I stay in the room for what feels like a long time. It could be a couple of hours. Then, unceremoniously, I simply say, "Okay, Dad. I gotta go."

We shake hands, and I say goodbye. His grip is still firm, but his fingers are boney and feel kind of separated. His once vice-like hands are still strong, but they now feel like vulture claws. I am even aware of his fingernails! Why does that hurt me worse than the boney skeleton I'm looking at?

As I drive my new-found friend's car back to the airport, I'm overly cautious. My thoughts are swimming and uncertain. I can't even focus on stop signs. Maneuvering through what little bit of traffic exists is difficult. I feel like I'm trying to slow down and be invisible while fleeing a crime scene. I can't wait to get in my plane and be back in the air. Oh, man, do I ever need real-world separation.

My brother Owen, lives just a few miles north of Annapolis on the shore of a quiet tributary to the Chesapeake Bay. He is a successful lawyer with a beautiful wife and a letter-perfect family. As I mentioned, he is also a lay preacher in the local and very popular Pentecostal Church. Quite frankly, I am simply not up to any form of Goodness and Mercy right now. I cannot get myself to make even a simple courtesy call to him. My flimsy justification is that my *not calling* will make things easier for both of us. What a wimpy excuse. In Owen's biblical eyes, Dad and I are both hell-bound anyway. Still, all this rambling and emotional pitch of mine is a weak defense for selfish discourtesy, isn't it? Well, so what? With respect to personal relationships, except for the service guy at the airport, I'm batting a perfect zero anyway. My stomach is growling, and just a fast-food hamburger with my brother would show at least a hint of character. But hell. I can hardly swallow just sitting here at a traffic light. Forget it.

When I step up on the Mooney wing and open the airplane door, the oily/musty-upholstery smell of my trusty old buddy here drifts out all over me like honey fresh out of the comb. Finally, there is no conflict. I can hardly wait until I detach the rest of my emotional connections from this lush Maryland fantasy.

On climb-out, I easily clear the trees and power lines at the west end of the runway. After a 90-degree departure bank to the south, I take my first deep, fresh, oxygen-filled breath of the day.

The Chesapeake Bay Bridge, Annapolis, Maryland

'Tis a Fool's Errand That Seeks a Bridge Too Far

Just a few miles farther north off the left wing, the graceful curve of the Bay Bridge makes its stately and sophisticated statement. What a perfect expression of beauty, logic, science, engineering, and aesthetic symmetry. It is proud, strong and elegant, yet it is also stoically unemotional. Man, I need some more of this. I ease around farther left to a northeast heading. As the Naval Academy comes up ahead, I bend a little farther south to stay out of their airspace. In a few minutes, I'm about a mile up-stream of the bridge on the Eastern Shore side. The graceful cables mimic the iconic Golden Gate Bridge in San Francisco. Holding altitude at a thousand feet, I catch a rare view of something lodged in the musical harp-like, vertical suspension cables supporting the elevated roadbed. It's a giant black whale with a large steel lockbox mounted to her back. Her nose is pointed directly at me, but I cannot see her eyes. In my mind, there is no question that she's caught in that giant net hanging from those two structural steel towers. In Watermen's jargon, this kind of vertical fishing net is called a seine. When I was a teenager, not twenty miles south of here, my uncle, Captain Lerch taught me how to *seine* this Bay for bait shrimp.

But right now, I am a prowling raptor perfectly positioned to help the quarry. I am her only friend. I have a mission. I can finally let go of all that father-son guilt and do something worthy!

This is a calling at exactly the right moment in my life. My cluttered brain finally drains of all the confusion of this morning's reality.

I ease back on the throttle and push the nose over. This wide, circular approach is working out nicely. The clearance between the Bay and the underside of the roadbed is over 150 feet. I'm 50 feet above the water. Clearance is not an issue. There is no sense of risk-taking. I'm now fulfilling my obligation to *save something*. This time it is a whale! Somehow this all feels so right!

As I cruise under the structure, I must now confess that the whale is not really a whale. Actually, it is a Nautilus Class submarine. Of course, I knew that when I first saw it, but sometimes mental multitasking is the only way to sort out emotional conflicts. The *submarine* is now at my two o'clock and a good distance away. It is only then that I realize that the activity I saw on her foredeck is, in reality, a fancy cocktail party in progress! It's a party boat! There are sweet smelling women in white, light-blue and pink frilly dresses mingling with ram-rod straight young men in crisp, white, dress uniforms. Several tables with white linen are set out with colorful flower centerpieces. The tantalizing canapés are only finger batons for the music I can't hear. But my errant mind still wonders how many of those women are thinking about those big circles in the deck right under their high heels. These are, of course, the exit hatches for the twelve intercontinental ballistic missiles. Each missile carries a nuclear warhead that could blow Annapolis all the way to Antarctica. And how about that little 'ole nuclear power plant back there in the stern? I figure it's probably turned off, and the party is running on its monster backup/ballast-batteries.

As I blow by at conning-tower height, in one coordinated movement, the deck-party attendees all look over at me. Because I don't want to look like a hostile intruder, I offer a friendly smile and wholehearted wave to my audience. *There is no response.* Snobs! We are too far away from each other to make eye contact. I can only see lots of blank faces. You gotta wonder what they're all saying to one another right now.

I know one thing for sure. Their brain waves and mine could not be further out of sync.

In a flash, this phase is over, and I'm starting to have some rational thoughts about the wisdom of this little episode. But the word *rational* hurts. Only moments ago, all this seemed so important. Unquestionably, the submarine has incredible radar capacity, and certainly the Naval Academy, which is only a mile or two over there, does too. Obviously, anonymity in saving whales is not the issue here. The real issue has to do with guilt, frustration, vengeance, and deliberate rule-breaking. I'm not sure why I'm here, except this is where I am. What might have started as an attempt to eclipse the frustration of a father-son failure has now escalated into a public display of abhorrent behavior.

I'm also beginning to feel like a fugitive. Gently, I ease the plane down a tad lower – to about 20 feet above the water. But there is no hiding out here.

Then it hits me: "This is crazy. What I just did was simply dumb as hell. And if I get caught, I get caught. It wasn't airmanship, and it wasn't derring-do. It was some sort of stupid shit that surfaced out of random mental flights of uncalled-for fantasy. This game is over! My guilt and I are heading to Atlanta. If I'm in trouble, best it be there."

I climb up to 8500 feet, set up for cruise speed, and head southwest into a setting sun.

The rest of the early evening is simply a beautiful flight south. I'm all alone with a big blue sky scattered with handfuls of white, cumulus build-ups

As I pointed out at the beginning of this flight, it is easy to see the whale caught in a steel suspension net. But here, as I fly between a white knight and the dark shadow of a rook of uncertain origin, I search desperately for a diagonal corridor from a black-topped bishop. I know it's out there somewhere. The next move is not as easy as you might think. To make everything work, some of the pieces must be negative spaces. But fortunately, because I'm playing both sides of the game, I can change the rules to suit the situation. Also, keep in mind this is not a game of *moves*. It's a game of *relationships*. Inflexible rules don't exist

15 of the 16 Dumbest Things I Have Ever Done in an Airplane

up here. From what I see before me, my first "relationship move" is obvious. Since they are not contributing to the suspense of battle, I disqualify all pawns from participating. Done. I'm now playing with only a few of the *royal row* delegates. Here, even after I flew into the middle of this gambit, it's still isn't doing what I want it to do.

And here's the crazy thing about sky-chess. The forgoing description didn't take 2 seconds to playout in my head. It's one of those flash-thoughts we all have all the time. I mean hundreds of times a day. You might be looking at a coconut custard pie in a restaurant window and completely replay when Aunt Hoosey taught you to make oatmeal when you were 7 years old. But if you don't record it, it's half-life is very short. Worthy or not, I elect to record sky-chess here only because it happened.

Without question, I feel fierce guilt by my personal response to my father's weakened physical condition followed by that ditzy bridge antic. Seeing the specter of my adolescence and adulthood now weak, old, and frail, brought me no satisfaction at all. But maybe it's really something worse. I call it guilt only because it is the lightest charge I can come up with. But even if it is only guilt, then what am I guilty of? I'm not sure.

But I know one thing for sure. I am guilty of flying under the bridge. As I said, that was simply stupid. But was it executed solely to materialize guilt? This should be easy to answer, but for me, I don't even know where to begin.

Right now, still here at altitude and by myself, as I look back on this whole day that I've just shared, I find that I have made a conspicuously slanted presentation here. The father-figure presented herein, except for his hospital gown, is addressed only in a dark color, and his character is presented accordingly gloomy. The son is presented otherwise. He enjoys waving to cocktail parties on a submarine deck, and then casually flies through some kind of static chess game in the clouds. So how balanced is that? Well, of course, it's not. Hell. Even I can see that.

I'm now over South Carolina and just waiting for the sun to finish setting so that I can fly in forgiving darkness with only sparkles, celestial or earthly to navigate by. An hour ago, in that chess game, I turned off the radios and electronic navigation systems. I still need more disconnect if I can find it.

Then, another conjecture pops up in my head. Could it be that my father waited for me to visit him so he could then die *complete*? The magnitude of the vanity in this unfettered expression of ego is so far off the scale that even I am embarrassed to share it here. But there it is.

I mean, who the hell do I think I am? Where are the boundaries of reality? Maybe death is reality's only defining edge. If so, which side of the edge is better? Socrates asked that very question just before he polished off the last of his hemlock. "The time for parting has come, each to take his way. I to die, you to live. Which is better? God only knows."

It's fully dark now and my mind is inching into that gloomy swamp again. I need to get back to flying. For this last 75 miles to Atlanta, I simply follow the red tail lights of cars and trucks on Interstate 85 going southwest. Using radios and electronic navigation this evening would only dilute today's disengagement from reality.

The night approach to PDK is easy as pie. The green and white blinking light is visible 20 miles out. I turn my radio back *on* to report-in to the tower. On short-final, however, the control tower calls to tell me to turn my landing lights on. I take that as a sign. Today is finally over. I turn'm on.

Driving home from the airport, at every turn, whether somebody is coming or not, I use my turn signals. Nobody ever does that. But all that hokey-pokey chess/death/reality stuff is now behind me. I'm finally starting to get back the security of that old, comfortable bump-and-grind of family, friends, and business.

The next morning, I get to my office early. Brother Owen calls me at 10 AM and tells me that our father died last night. My first thought is that I never did tell him that I loved him. Now how damned hypocritical is that? My only excuse is that I'm positively certain that I never told him that in my life – probably because I never thought that I did.

But do you know what's really scary? As I write all this down, I see some, but not all, of my father's qualities in myself. That's the way these things always happen, isn't it?

I clear my calendar for the next four days and call Nancy to get the family ready to fly back to DC for the funeral. She needs another day to get the kids and her business in order. I drive back to PDK alone. Since the weather is forecast to be rainy and overcast, I file an instrument flight plan to Washington National Airport. In the box for "number of souls on board," I put a "1." The imperfection of that one soul makes me wonder if even that isn't an exaggeration. I wonder what would happen if I put in a zero.

Ten years ago, I made this same trip, in this same plane, again alone, to the same DCA airport. It was in the same bad weather, but that time it was to attend my mother's funeral. I cried almost the whole way up there. Crying while you're flying is like trying to breathe through a Snorkel clogged with popcorn. It can be done, but …

For Dad's ceremony, I cried not a drop en route and still arrived two days early. My buddy, Pat Epps, volunteered to fly

Nancy and the kids up there the next day in his twin-engine Navajo.

The funeral services are in a small chapel in the middle of the large and quietly elegant Fort Lincoln Cemetery. Owen stands at the pulpit and expresses his Christian beliefs with pastoral conviction. The message is about how and where he thinks we each will spend eternity. His best friend, another evangelical preacher, is next at the lectern and faithfully reinforces the message.

After the two otherworldly professionals have presented their views on death and eternal life, I feel compelled to offer another perspective. This is fine, except I have neither knowledge nor clear conviction about how we humans actually make it through the rest of eternity.

When it's my time to speak, I walk up to the pulpit and in a strategic move of desperation, start my pitch by asking each of the twenty or so mourners to say something nice about Dad. This gives me a little time to think of something to say. As each person is improvising, I hear almost nothing of their comments. My mind skips around for some quick quip of wisdom, but nothing comes up. Finally, after we've run out of personal testimonies, ready or not, it's my turn. I end up walking around the pulpit to a funeral bouquet on guard duty behind the casket. It is a ceremonial vase full of traditional funeral flowers and greenery. Its only distinction is that within a cluster of colorful petals and ferns are a half dozen cattails. At first glance, the flowerless, inelegant, brown hot dogs-on-a-stick are out of character here. I pull one cattail out from the bunch and to use as a metaphor for my father's life. I say something about it being the only un-blossomed, unscented, unadorned, uncolored contribution to an otherwise pungent cluster of floral arrays gathered around this tribute. Then I point out that when it's time for a cattail to blossom, this plain old brown seedpod simply explodes into gentle wisps of windblown feathers that put all the "pretty" flowers, with their now limp, faded, stinky-wilted petals to shame. The cattail feathers go airborne to who knows where. I continue by stating that the cattail needs neither butterflies nor honeybees to survive. They just do it all themselves. Or something like that.

But the lasting question herein is whether this little impromptu salute to one man stirred anyone's perspective of life. Of course, the answer is an obvious, *yes*. It stirred mine.

We all had our personal link with Dad. And like a seed in a cattail pod, each connection had a set of wings – including his and mine.

Probably the greatest value of the spontaneous cattail metaphor was that it was simply the best I could do. As an incredible imperfect man as I am, I can only hope that this counts.

CHAPTER 5

Zero-Zero

> Zero-Zero (adj.) Definition:
> Having or characterized by zero
> visibility in both horizontal and
> vertical directions

BACK IN THE good old days, zero-zero landings were not what pilots planned for in advance. They happened because of inaccurate weather forecasts, sloppy flight management, bad luck, bad judgement or Mother Nature simply reminding everybody who still runs the show around here.

Currently, in filing a flight plan to an airport with iffy weather, the FAA rules help the situation considerably. Reduced to conversational English, it goes something like this; *If one's primary destination airport is forecast with less than visual landing minimums, you must file for an instrument landing. You must also select an alternate (backup) airport within a comfortable range, and with significantly better forecast conditions.* Consequently, if you follow these rules and read all the regulations of fine print (that I didn't show here), and keep your nose to the grindstone, there is almost no reason to ever have to make a zero-zero landing.

Oh, but if life were always so simple. To prove this point, permit me to invite your critical judgment of the following event. It took place in Atlanta, Georgia on November 27, 1976. My log book at the time indicated that I had a little over 2000 hours as PIC and held an instrument/commercial/multiengine pilot's license.

A few days ago, Nancy and our baby daughter, Lee, and I had flown our Mooney down to Sarasota, Florida for a weekend visit with friends. It's now Sunday and we're headed back to Atlanta. An hour ago, I checked with FAA Flight Service. The weather in ATL is lousy. It's that zero-zero stuff I just mentioned. The good news, however, is that this weather is forecast to lift to visual conditions *in an hour.* That's what morning fogs do down South. By the time we take off, the low ceiling should have already lifted. I file an Instrument Flight Plan anyway. It calls for a little over 3 hours en route. From the time of my call, this will give Mother Nature a full *four hours* to clear things up before our arrival. On top of that, and because of my precious cargo of beautiful women, I add another layer of safety. We will fly at slow cruise, 135 mph rather than our normal 155 mph. This will add another half hour to the trip, but it offers the weather-gods even more time to clean up their act. Moreover, the cloud ceiling at our destination airport doesn't need to lift but 200 feet to make it legal for us land there on instruments. Still, you can't be too careful, you know.

In filing our instrument flight plan, I selected Chattanooga, Tennessee, as our alternate airport. If we should need it, which of course we won't, this would add another 100 miles to the trip.

The Mooney has about a 5-hour fuel duration. Winds aloft for our trip are forecast light and variable. This means that there is no meaningful headwind to contend with. At midmorning, we hug our weekend hosts farewell, load up, and we're on our way.

We plan to be home for lunch.

The initial flight conditions up through North Florida and South Georgia turn out to be an easy in between cloud trip with hardly noticeable little ripples every now and then. Radio contact with Air Traffic Controllers along the way makes the trip safe, comfortable, and friendly. Nancy always brings along snacks and goodies on our flights, so we just nibble our way north. Still, as a pilot herself, she can't help but keep an eye on everything-aviation going on. When I tell her we're going to fly at econo-cruise speed, she doesn't need to ask why. She knows it's a timing and fuel management process.

About an hour south of Atlanta, we're coming up on Macon, Georgia. Just to confirm that the meteorological conditions in Atlanta have performed as forecast, I radio Flight Service for an updated weather report. It turns out that, no; Atlanta is still zero-zero. Hmm. This can't be right. The complexion of this whole trip changes from fat margins of safety to regular margins. Considering my passenger manifest, this is not what I want.

I slow our air speed down to 110 mph – not quite the cruise speed of a two-seat Cessna trainer. Almost an hour later, as we approach Atlanta's airspace, I sense a conspicuous dearth of aircraft chatter on the radio. The cloudy undercast blanketing the earth below us looks like a cushy feather-comforter that goes from horizon to horizon. When Air Traffic Control passes us off to Atlanta Approach Control, I ask about the paucity of air traffic transmissions. I don't use "paucity," but they reply that Atlanta Hartsville International Airport *is closed* to commercial traffic! All landing traffic is either in holding patterns or they have been vectored off to their alternate airports. *Both ceiling and visibility at ATL are currently zero-zero.*

I'm thinking, *Well, damn.* Yes, we still have enough fuel to reach our alternate airport with our required forty-five-minute reserve, but that's about it. Because the weather isn't moving out as predicted, I check on the Chattanooga Metropolitan Airport (CHA) weather just to be sure they are still eligible as an alternate choice. Flight Service radio responds that the entire weather system in Georgia and Tennessee has stalled, and Chattanooga is now below minimum required instrument landing conditions. *It is no longer an eligible alternate airport.* Flight Service then adds, however, that CHA weather is expected to lift within an hour. If it does, it will then become eligible again, just before we get there.

Well, double damn! "Lifting within an hour" sounds like what Atlanta was forecast to do *four hours ago.* I call Flight Service again to ask for some other airport options. Greenville, North Carolina, sounds best, so I pick it. It's 40 miles farther away than Chattanooga, but in a northeast direction. Technically, it meets FAA *visibility minimums* but not the fuel-reserve minimums. This puts it at our fuel limit. If we select it, we will have to land there regardless of the weather.

Also, of note, the slightest ill wind can throw all of these calculations out of kilter. If things continue going in the wrong direction, the question will become, "How ill is the wind?" And, more importantly, "how accurate are my fuel consumption estimates?"

This "accuracy concept" keeps swirling around in my head. Consider this: I have been flying my family for nearly four hours; much of the last hour on solid instruments. This plane has neither autopilot nor wing-levelers to offer the pilot the privilege of a few minutes to spread out charts with both hands, use scaled rulers, write notes on fuel consumption, measure accurate distances traveled (or anticipated), or even to locate exactly where we are on an aviation chart. We have not seen Mother Earth since Macon, Georgia. Fuel consumption in gallons per hour is only an estimate – call it an educated guess. Distances traveled (or planned) are conjecture as well. Yes, I have my slide rule with me, and I'm well-practiced in its use. But it still takes two hands to operate it. Flying the airplane requires one of them. Collectively, all the unknowns in this situation have become considerable. My trust in forecast weather predictions, however, is at an incredibly low ebb.

This is not a flight school drill. It has become a life-and-death drama.

There is nothing I can do now except play this game out to the end. I can only keep making judgments and base my next decision on what appears to be the best choice.

Commercial airliners are *not* permitted to even attempt an approach to an airport whose current weather is below published landing minimums. Private aircraft, however, *are* permitted this privilege.

Dead calm weather is normally what we have in the mornings before the sun starts heating things up to get local weather systems percolating. It's now mid-afternoon. I find it hard to believe that the ceiling and visibility are still zeros this late in the day. I'm confident enough of this meteorological tradition that I then call Approach Control to set us up for an approach into our home field, Peachtree Airport. There is little question in my mind that the weather there is lifting and breaking up. This is simply the way these things work. Approach Control obligingly gives me headings to line up on the ILS (Instrument Landing System) and hands us over to Peachtree Tower radio.

Fifteen miles out, we're lined up on the ILS radio beams. This navigation indicator has two needles. The position of the horizontal needle indicates if we're above or below an invisible downhill, electronic path to the runway. This is called a Glide Slope. The vertical needle on this gauge indicates if we are right or left of the centerline of that path. This is called a Localizer. If we keep both needles centered, we'll descend right down the middle of the intersection of these two beams to the runway. For safety's sake, however, regulations say that if we don't see the airport when we get down to 200 feet of altitude above the ground, we must then stop our descent and declare a "Missed Approach." The Tower will then give us headings and altitudes to our alternate airport.

That's a thumbnail of the procedure. But right now, Approach Control is finishing vectoring us to get into position to start the approach. They then hand us over to the Tower. After locking the two needles on to the glide path, we start sliding right down to the 200-foot minimum. We reach that point and Nancy has not called sighting the earth below. I stop the descent, level the plane out, and look up from the instrument panel. There is not a whisper of terra firma out there anywhere. There is nothing outside this airplane but wall-to-wall potato soup.

I guess I was wrong about weather traditions.

I radio "missed approach" to the Tower and ease in the throttle control. We start a climb back up to 3,000 feet and begin the procedure to fly to Greenville, NC.

Just as I'm starting this new program, another notion crosses my mind. Fulton County Airport (FTY) is only ten minutes to the west of here. Their field elevation is *150 feet lower* than PDK. Because they are down in the Chattahoochee River basin, weather conditions there are frequently significantly different from that at Peachtree. I am still concerned about having enough fuel to get to Greenville. As I said, the time and distance for us to get there work out, but just barely. And the truth is, the plan is not worked out *on paper*. It is worked out in my head while I'm trying to maintain assigned altitudes, read instrument approach plates, keep on exact headings, and maintain intelligent conversations with Air Traffic Control.

None the less, in a snap decision, I call Atlanta Approach Control again and request an ILS approach into Fulton County Airport. They are only 20 miles away and I have made their approach many times – including the flight test for my Instrument Rating.

Obligingly, Approach Control vectors us out west of the city to line us up on the FTY approach. This is the same procedure we just went through at PDK. By the time they have turned us around to return to FTY, they have vectored us out some 20 or 30 miles farther away from Greenville. The total of all the distances of this approach – when added to the last one – is starting to total-up to perhaps 50 to 70 miles that I had not figured on. This, in turn, adds maybe another thirty minutes of flying time. This time was not calculated in my new selection of Greenville as our emergency alternate airport. Again, this reinforces the fact that our flight to Greenville will become a dead-end trip. We will have no choice but to land at that airport whether we can see it or not.

Given all the information I've been able to garner, I don't feel that any of the decisions or calculations I've made so far are outside the approved protocol of normal flight planning. But the vagaries of my approximations, coupled with the variables of nature, and the inaccuracy of FAA predictions, are all starting to make this situation a witch's brew of uncertainty. And, as everyone knows, *uncertainty* in times of stress, is a very dangerous bedfellow.

As I swing the plane around to line up on the invisible Fulton County radio beams, I can feel my brain dialed into its keenest edge. This feels good. Descending down the glideslope, I obediently maneuver up and down and left and right and keep both needles' dead-centered perfectly.

15 OF THE 16 DUMBEST THINGS I HAVE EVER DONE IN AN AIRPLANE

The control of the plane feels clean and exact. The uncommonly static-calm-weather permits me to stay locked in solid to the navigating signals. My whole world is no larger than that 3-inch diameter artificial horizon instrument right in front of my nose. It has the airspeed indicator on one side and the altimeter on the other. Of course, both the heading indicator and glide slope also play close harmony in this quintet. I dare not look at any of these instruments for more than one second. My eyes keep dancing so that not one of them has a chance to wander.

There is no sense of fear or apprehension. So far, this approach has been letter-perfect. As I said, there is neither a crosswind nor a breath of turbulence. I am sealed in a capsule of immobile space. Nothing on the panel is moving except the altimeter and the second hand on the clock. In fact, watching the ILS needles locked into position makes me want to flip the navigation frequency selector for just a second, just to be certain it's working. But everything is so perfectly balanced that this is not the time to start testing anything. I must simply trust what I've done so far. I'm so focused on keeping the glide slope and localizer needles centered that I'm now concerned that my mind might start to close off the other instruments.

Yes, I know, complacent certainty is not a good place to be either. Flying is *never* about doing one thing perfectly. To get out of this isolation booth, I force myself to step out of my head and watch what's going on from over my own shoulder. This feels better. I'm now monitoring the entire approach as opposed to just being a glide-slope operator. I can now see Nancy in the seat next to me. She's holding Lee and looking out the copilot window. And me, I'm leaning too far forward into the instruments. I settle back a little. Still erect, I stretch my shoulders and force relaxation. The posture shift helps.

Exactly at the radio beep of the Outer-Marker beacon, I slow down to 90 miles per hour and lower the landing gear. The

Outer-Marker beep signals that we're 15 miles from the airport. It also reinforces that we are exactly where we're supposed to be! This is a huge confidence builder. I watch myself take a big breath and rack my shoulders again.

Then the Middle Marker radio signal beeps. These radio markers are electronic beacons like vertical searchlights on the ground directly below the glide-slope beam that indicate the waypoint distances to the threshold of the runway. We're now 6.1 miles out from the runway threshold we can't see yet. I slow to 80 mph and pump in full flaps and retrim the plane. It takes almost twenty seconds for the plane to resettle. When it stabilizes, I then slow down to 70 miles per hour. But this time, I don't retrim. Keeping a little back-pressure on the control wheel makes me feel like I'm now physically holding the plane on the glide slope. I don't want completely neutral controls. Seventy is slow, but the plane still feels solid. We're 13 mph above stall speed.

There is still not a hint of turbulence. I want to fly as slow as possible because the moment I see the runway, I'm going to cut the engine-power completely and land quickly. There may not be time to bleed off any extra airspeed.

The altimeter winds down to 1040 feet; This is exactly 200 feet above the runway. It's called Decision Height. This is as low as we are approved to go. I glance out the window for the runway. This peep cannot take but one second – max.

Nothing. I can't believe it!

I then let the altimeter gently ease down to 940 feet. This is called *cheating*. I glance up again. Still no runway. Both glide-slope needles are still rock-solid dead center. Everything being so exactly right-on brings on my first flash-shadow of nervousness. This cheating on the glide slope beam is a new experience for me.

Should I go a little bit lower? Do I still have enough fuel to get to Greenville?

This suspended animation period is only a few seconds, but that's long enough!

That's it! I ease in on the power and gently raise the nose to start to climb out cautiously.

Because we're flying so slow, except in an emergency, any change in our flying configuration must be butter-smooth. Next to me, only inches away, breathe the two greatest loves of my life. So far, except for the 100-foot cheat, this approach has been executed precisely as prescribed. I will not screw it up now!

As I said, Nancy knows everything that's going on, and Lee is the blessed embodiment of our two lives. Every evening when I come home, she jumps up for me to catch her, and then she hangs on to my neck with what we call "The Big Hug." And I always say, "Not that big!" She then yells "Daddy" like I'm the biggest event in the history of humankind. Right now, just as she's been for the last hour, she's being clamped/smothered in the soft power-vice of her mother's arms. She's also been uncharacteristically silent for that hour. Not a sigh nor a whimper. This is not her nature. How does she know?

According to the instruments, we're still level at 100 feet above ground level. We're below decision height. We're still flying. My decision is absolute. *I continue to bring the throttle up to start our Missed Approach.*

Just then– RUMP! Bumble-bumple-bumple. We contact the earth! Solid, but no bounce! I catch a glimpse of one runway light passing off the left wing-tip and pull the engine throttle back to full-off. Then I flip the retract switch for the wing flaps to *plant* the plane and get on the brakes firmly. These actions take only a fraction of the time it took you to read that sentence. I'm super careful not to lock up the brakes. We decelerate straight ahead to an unremarkable stop on the centerline of a wet but solid runway. I am in wonder as to how that happened so quickly and how I was able to react accordingly. It was not my intent and it doesn't seem possible. When we stop rolling, everything's solemnly quiet. The engine is ticking over at a lazy idle.

I look over at Nancy. She looks straight back. Two eyes to two eyes. No blinking. No hatred. No anger. No great sigh of relief. I think she might release enough pressure on Lee so that the two of them can breathe again. Without words between Nancy and me, there is a micro-second of nuclear communication – there just aren't any words.

But words do come over the radio, "Mooney-one, nine, two, eight, yankee, Fulton Tower. What is your situation?" There is tension in the Tower operator's voice.

Probably, they are looking for me to call "Missed approach."

I answer, "We're on the runway."

They reply, "Fulton Tower. We do not have you in sight. State your intentions."

"We're taxiing over to the base of the tower and will park there."

Tower: "How about a ceiling report on the weather west of the airport."

"There were breaks in the clouds." I just leave it at that.

As I said, I've landed here many times before. The airport layout is comfortable and familiar. We taxi slowly along the painted centerline of the runway, turn right, then right again, and we're on the taxiway back to the control tower we can't see yet. Obviously, visibility is not zero. It is probably more like 80 or 100 feet.

From the terminal lobby, I call a taxicab, and we're home within an hour. All safe and sound.

This brief event becomes a useful sounding board for probing questions like, "Was the flight planning adequate? Was the execution of the decision-making process appropriate to the circumstances? Was a landing below minimums necessary? Should we have obediently gone straight to Greenville *and not* made the approaches into both PDK and Fulton County? What else should I have done differently?" As with so many choices and decisions we make in life, there will always be some that we cannot appraise until after the action part has played itself out.

However, no matter what the verdict is concerning this incident, I do not exonerate myself from not flawlessly executing all the privileges of my pilot's license. In my defense, however, I must say that this little event was not a planned act of derring-do. I was caught up in a series of unknown circumstances that required immediate and deliberate reaction. I responded to the best of my ability and judgment. I share this incident now, decades later, only as an example that sometimes situations, both real and imagined, can build to a point outside the normal set of house rules. It is then up to the participants to make judgments. And, as you know, individual judgments are always fair game for outside critics.

If this is so, then my next question is, "Would you, as a pilot, choose to be fluent in the language of *personal response to a given procedure*, or would you prefer to always keep faithful to *blind obedience to rules and rote*?"

Since you didn't peep up, I'll give you a clue. They both have their strengths, but occasionally there will be a blurry area between them. Consequently, you as an individual must tilt to whichever flavor suits your nature. However, being loyal to your personal code and respecting the other will nearly always yield the most favorable outcome. Even if your choice costs you dearly.

CHAPTER 6

Back-Seat Driver

IN THE AVIATION community, the Mooney Super-21 has a reputation for being something of a little sportscar of an airplane. It's smallish, fastish, lightish, noisyish and wonderfully fuel efficient. Consequently, its flight-handling characteristics are distinctively different from Cessnas, Pipers, or Beechcrafts. In my experience the Mooney's elevator reaction-time is quicker, and the aileron response seems a little slower than the other brands.

Also, in ordinary, everyday, level flight, my old Super 21 tends to always search for a proper, stable cruise speed. It's not a big thing. We're only talking about a couple of knots, plus or minus. But there is definitely something going on in there worth studying.

Possibly to address this edgy issue, nearly all new Mooneys come from the factory with either full autopilots or semi-autopilots called *wing levelers*. For some reason, the first owner of my plane ordered her with no such woosie-assist equipment. My trusty steed is just unfettered, no-flying-assist, raw Mooney. I don't know whether the autopilot solves the cruise speed problem or not, but for sure, it would probably help.

15 of the 16 Dumbest Things I Have Ever Done in an Airplane

When making long cross-country trips, however, no matter how nifty the ship you sail, sometimes the captain's natural curiosity will search for a measure of mental engagement just to justify its existence. The issue of variable cruise settings for optimal airspeeds at different altitudes and temperatures is a healthy diversion. All pilots do it. Experimentation is just part of the job description. Isn't it the tinkering with all relationships that keeps them alive?

For this particular tinker, my 'ole Mooney and I left Jamaica about an hour ago. We're solo-bound for Barranquilla, Colombia. From there, we plan to fly up into the Andes Mountains to Bogotá, Colombia where I'll set up an architectural office to design an office building for an old college chum's father-in-law.

This particular leg of the trip is a long five-hour flight that runs north–south across the Caribbean Sea. Within forty minutes, we're out of all communication and navigation range of the civilized world. There is nothing to do now but sit here holding 225 degrees on the magnetic compass and maintaining 12,000 feet on the altimeter. To make it even lonelier, the weather is crystal clear with long vistas of Mother Earth's endless oceanic splendor spreading out in all directions. The oversized sky makes the Mooney and me feel damn-near subatomic. Time ticks by. Nowhere in the unspoiled sea below us is there even a hint of a ship or even its left-over wake to help stoke memories of back when we were part of civilized world.

To reduce the burden of all this exquisite nothing-going-on, I put on my instrument training hood. The hood itself is like a black, lightweight, welder's helmet – except the black glass is missing so that you have a cone of forward vision of only the instrument panel directly in front of your nose. Peripheral vision of the horizon outside the airplane is completely obscured. Flying "under the hood" simulates flying in clouds so thick that, except with respect to the instruments, the pilot cannot see which way is up,. Customarily, the hood is used only with an instrument instructor sitting in the right seat criticizing everything the pilot is doing – right or wrong. This critic also watches out for other air traffic. Flying without a spotter over this immense, undisturbed absence of fellow man's existence carries virtually zero risk of conflict with other traffic.

As I'm flying along "under the hood," time ticks by. My mind is now totally consumed with the small-screen view of the instrument gauges. Then, after a half an hour or so, WAMPLE! WAMBLE! WAMPLE! The plane starts a violent shudder! The normal slipstream noise turns into a roar! The control wheel in my hand vibrates strangely! We've hit something! In one whip-motion, I flip the hood off into the rear seat. A flash-scan of the windshield, wings, prop, and instrument panel all reveal absolutely nothing in disorder. But the landing gear warning light on the panel is showing *green*. In flight, with the gear up, it's supposed to be red.

The landing gear extension and retraction bar is a hand-operated lever called a Johnson Bar between the two front seats. When I reach down to check that the lever is still properly locked-in-place, my hand hits my battalion-sized, military binoculars. It seems that they have vibrated over from the right seat and fallen, tripping the latch that secures the Johnson Bar in its bracket. This action knocked the latching clip open, which in turn, released the wheels from their tucked-up position in the wings. I push the Bar back down in place and relatch it. That quickly, the world is again back to normal. After everything settles down, (most particularly, my heart rate,) my conclusion is that flying solo *under the hood* invites vagaries of uncertainty not conducive to peaceful flight. I make a personal vow that without a spotter-pilot with me, I'll not do that again. Period. End of lesson.

The long, lonely flight resumes. There are still hours to go. I again scan the sea for ships' wakes – still none. So, here I am, back to just humming along, pretending nothing happened.

One might think that a little landing gear experience like this last one might quell the percolating curiosity of a long, untaxing flight – mightn't one? I should be so lucky.

That ever-annoying *curiosity bug* now reawakens and alights on that unstable cruise speed characteristic of this plane that I mentioned earlier.

A little more carefully explained – at cruise settings, after everything is all set up at a selected altitude, the airspeed of this ship will hold steady for several minutes. Then the plane will gradually slow 2 or 3 knots and hang at that speed until I go through a whole new trim setup routine.

My speculation is that there is something out of kilter in either the weight-and-balance configuration or in the elevator-trim alignment of the plane. The Mooney doesn't use trim tabs along the trailing edge of their elevator as most other planes do. The Mooney rotates the whole tail assembly (rudder and horizontal stabilizer) on a horizontal pivot-point in the fuselage just a little forward of the rudder.

While in flight, obviously, there is not much one can do with the adjustment of any internal mechanics of the elevator mechanism. Consequently, this morning, I am restricted to focusing my attention on simple weight-and-balance experiments.

The weight of an airplane is divided into two categories: (1.) empty weight, and (2.) live load. Empty weight is whatever comes off the assembly line at the factory. Live load is whatever cargo, fuel, pilot, crew, and anything else you add for the purpose of the flight.

Obviously, right now the biggest live-load mass I can work with is the 190-pound pilot sitting in the front left seat. If I can get that moveable and willing live load relocated another 3 feet further aft – say, to the back seat – the new moment-arm from the center of lift *may* eliminate the plane's *searching for the cruise-balance* point. But it might make things worse. As they say, there is one way to find out. And right now, with absolutely nothing else going on, it sorta sounds like we don't have much choice, does it? Besides, you don't need to wear a training hood to do this experiment.

The first order of business, for any little project like this, is to do a little housekeeping. All the junk I've carelessly spread around in the cockpit is put in its respective place of order. Charts get properly folded and slipped into their packets, which, in turn, go numerically in the flight case. The flight case is then closed, latched, and put out of the way on the copilot's floor. Pencils all go in their holders and beer cans out the window … no, no, just kidding about the beer cans! That's just me trying to take the edge off of too much administrative detail. Please keep in mind: what we're trying here is not hard science. We're only doing a little in-the-field experiment just to keep our long-haul, brain-jelly from setting up like it sometimes wants to.

Next on our duty roster is to create as much crew circulation space between the two front seats and the back bench seat as possible. This *is* important. I slide the right seat as far forward as it will go, then tip its seat-back forward. I'm careful that it does not conflict with the copilot control wheel. If things do not go as planned, and should I feel an immediate need to get back in the pilot's seat quickly, this pathway forward is critical. Just think about climbing from the back seat of the family Honda Civic, up to driver's seat while you're on an interstate highway at three times the speed limit. Because the Mooney locates its landing gear lever and the nose-trim wheel between the front seats, there must remain a couple of built-in obstacles.

The plane continues humming along comfortably. But I can sense it watching me prepare to make the next move.

After I let it build up a little impatience, I slide my pilot seat all the way back to its rear stop and check to be certain it's latched in place. I don't want it to move an inch until I want it to. *Shifting weight cautiously* is the name of the next move. Before moving myself aft, I set the engine RPMs, manifold pressure, and the exhaust gas temperature gauge (EGT) to perfection. Then I switch the fuel selector to the fuller tank. We don't need any surprise engine stumbling while we're out of the office. Then I adjust the nose trim forward to a descent rate of 200 feet per minute. Too little *nose-down* is probably better than too much. I want to be confident that we will start climbing once I undertake the load shift to the back seat. The big unknown right now is how much climb-effect the weight-shift will make.

The change in the balance of the plane will be the three feet that I will move my butt to the rear. Thee-feet times 190 pounds is 570 foot-pounds. Is this a lot or a little? Who knows? But think about it this way. If you have a box-end wrench with a one-foot handle, and you hook it onto a nut and pull with 100 pounds of muscle, you've developed 100 foot-pounds of force. Moving my body to the back seat is almost six times that much. Five hundred and seventy foot-pounds sound like a lot to me.

Should anything in this weight-shift experiment go awry, I will definitely want to be able to scurry forward to the driver's seat with as little conflict as posible. I'm confident that saving a slow-climbing airplane will feel much more gratifying than moving my weight forward in an airplane that is already in an accelerating nosedive.

Okay. Enough speculation.

I shift my 190 pounds over between the two front seats and then scoot aft butt-first with my arms. Keeping my feet forward feels right too, especially if you're an oversized guy like me, 6'-2". Once set up in the back seat, obviously, I don't buckle in.

As I am scooting aft, the nose of the plane starts inching up. But it's not as aggressively as I feared. I take my time moving, and start trimming the nose down. After a couple of minutes, everything starts to feel within the bounds of control. It takes perhaps another five minutes for me to feel a measure of confidence about the situation.

Weight-shifting to bank left and right is obvious. You lean, and the plane obeys. What becomes most interesting now is how slow the lag time is. Adjusting to slo-mo input becomes the pilot-test of the afternoon. Eventually, once you're finally trimmed up, if you give it time, simply moving one arm left or right will start a responsive reaction. I try to get it down to using just a couple of fingers, but I'm too impatient to wait it out. Can you believe that?

Once everything has fairly well settled down to the straight and level again, it's the difference between fore and aft lag-time and right and left that becomes the sticky wicket. But they share one thing in common: *when the plane starts to comply to your initial input, do not wait to see how things are going to go. Immediately start neutralizing that first movement.* This goes especially for fore-and-aft weight shifts. Maintaining a constant *altitude* is several times more challenging than holding a *heading*.

Initially, I did my balancing act in the wrong sequence. I suggest that one should address altitude control first. As I said, the up-and-down nose-trim wheel is located between the two front seats right next to the landing gear Johnson Bar. The way to trim the nose down is to rotate the top of the trim wheel forward. To trim the airplane to climb, you roll the top of the wheel to the rear. In *back-seat flying*, obviously you do not want to lean forward to do this, you use your foot. The pressure to operate the nose-trim control wheel in the Mooney is so super-sensitive that I take off my left shoe *and sock* to feel the friction a little better. As it turns out, it is the position of the foot on the nose-trim wheel that will determine how and where you're going to occupy the back seat. When you first sit down back there, start by placing your foot on the trim wheel and then position the rest of the body accordingly.

Back to weight and balance numbers. Stretching the foot forward to the trim wheel considerably lessens the length of the moment arm caused by moving your body to the back seat. But lessening this moment-arm by maybe as much as 25 percent is probably not a bad idea. In other words, by reclining out as I suggest, the moment arm of the body is lessened by almost half.

Well, that's about it. You are now ready to be a back-seat driver. Now there's nothing left for you to do but start building some back-seat time and sharing your stories in your favorite pilot lounge. Right?

But I'll tell you right now what's going to happen. Surer'n the dickens, there is going to be someone there who hears you blowing all this smoke about flying from the rear pew with moment-arms dangling and will ask you something like, "Okay, now you told us how to do it. So what? For what earthly reason would you want to get into all this stuff?"

This is what you've been waiting for. Your brain double-clutches down a gear, and you answer, "I'm in the back seat because this is the only way I can get the plane to fly *on the step*." She's still watching you and looks skeptical. She asks, "What do you mean by '*on the step*?' I've never heard that term before." Her eyes are pretty, but the way she engages you tells you she's been around.

You've got to keep going almost like you expected the question. "Flying on the step is finding an extremely sensitive, fore-and-aft balancing point that reduces drag on the airplane. Think of it as 'the sweet spot.' If you can find this spot, it will add an extra three to four knots to your sustained cruise airspeed."

If you're lucky, she'll then look at you more closely and say, "Interesting. Okay, now tell me how that works."

That's it! You and Miss Starry Eyes are now locked on the same frequency. It's now time for you to wax professorial. You lean back and take a microsecond to check those eyes again. If *it's* still there, you stay on your A-game. You start with something like, "With only the pilot sitting in the plane, the CG is at, or a little forward of the center-of-lift point of the wings. Planes are designed this way so that you can add passengers in the backseat and stay within the weight-and-balance envelope. Consequently, with just the pilot on board, the elevator must provide a little *downforce* to keep the nose up and the plane level. And, as you know, in lift diagrams, downforce arrows increase drag. To get any bonus speed, the idea is to move the *live load*[7] weight in the plane as close as you can to the center of lift of the plane. Once you've done this, the plane's wing and horizontal stabilizer will be in perfect alignment with level flight at your altitude. Then, if you move your CG only slightly more-aft, say just an inch aft of the point of lift of the wing, this will require just the littlest amount of *lift* of the elevator in the tail of the plane to keep everything level. That little bit of uplift adds just a smidgeon of speed. The plane is now at its most perfect angle of attack. You're now flying *on the step.*"

If she hasn't already excused herself to go do whatever people go do when they don't buy your song and dance, she might say (with eyes still wide in wonder), "Really?"

---

[7] Live load = pilot, passengers, baggage, fuel, cargo, and anything else added. An early model twin-engine Beechcraft Baron with full fuel could not be flown legally with only one front-seat person of average size. This was not enough weight to bring the live load into the CG envelope. One could either unload some fuel or add a front seat passenger/copilot to be legal.

Now that you've gotten this far, (and she's studying you with keener eyes yet), she might even think kind thoughts concerning your approach to science and the order of things. From this point forward, everything between the two of you is simple chemistry. I have nothing further to offer either one of you except, "Good luck."

By the way, I did get my additional 3 knots of sustained cruise speed. But that is not the driving force behind this little experiment.

To address the "why do it" issue, permit me to pose another question, "Is it worth the sacrifice of comfort and safety to find a couple of knots of elusive airspeed?" The answer should go something like this: "Almost any exercise of the inquisitive mind will provide its own set of rewards. For some, sharing them here in the safety of the written word is one of them. For other minds, cerebral satisfaction is simply not enough. True gratification only comes from the culmination of a physical act."

DISCLAIMER: The weight and balance/flying-on-the-step theory proposed herein is entirely the mental machinations of myself. Other than my own experience as offered herein, it has no aeronautical engineering substantiation that I have ever heard of. I offer it here simply as an example of an inquisitive mind with a little time to spare.

CHAPTER 7

Open-Door Policy

AFTER MORE THAN ten years of a faithful and trusting relationship between my old four-seat Mooney and our four-member family, daughter Ruthie came along. Almost simultaneously, a good friend we call Zip was selling his well-used, six-seat Bonanza. We made a deal. After a new paint job, a fresh engine and refurbished interior, it was still not as bright and beautiful as Ruthie, but it still showed off its class and utility handsomely.

Oh, the sacrifices daddies have to make for their families.

The four seats in the back-cabin of the Bonanza faced each other with a small fold-out table to play games on, eat snacks and make noise and messes. It was like a micro-family room. It even had its own separate double-door entry. Nancy would sometimes sit back there with two of the kids, and I would have the third up front in the cockpit with me. Because they could not yet see over the instrument panel, I would teach them to fly with only the artificial horizon, altimeter and airspeed instruments. It would take a couple of more years before they would transition from the instrument panel up to the grown-up's horizon out there somewhere on the edge of their imagination.

The Bonanza was faster, quieter, and easier to fly than the Mooney. But nothing made by man is ever without a hiccup.

Case in point:

On a solo business trip from Atlanta down to Savannah, I leveled out at 7500 feet in smooth, clear air. Then, as I throttled back from climb power to cruise, *PA FOP!* followed by a steady roar. First thought – we hit something! We're too high for birds. It's gotta be another plane. But almost instantly, I see that the front passenger door has just popped ajar. It's on the other side of the copilot seat,

The roaring slipstream is sucking the door out four inches from the rear jamb. The noise is alarmingly loud, but the wind-sources inside the plane are swishy and nonturbulent. It's not like I'm about to be sucked out or anything. Mostly, the cockpit is just noisy as hell. When I reach across the cabin to pull the door closed, it will only come as close as an inch of latching, and that's it. Even with the plane on autopilot and using both hands, the door stops firmly at an inch open. Without the fear of pulling the handle off the door, it cannot be muscled shut. I try again with a reduced speed of 100 mph. This makes no discernible difference. I try 80. Slower speed calms the noise down a little bit, but makes no meaningful difference in getting the door any closer to latching.

The idea of giving away all this wonderful altitude to land at some nowhere airport for 3 seconds, just so I can close a door properly, seems like an awful lot of work for such a minimal return. Besides, the door being ajar isn't hurting anything. I give some thought to just leaving it as is, but the distractions and commotion are ruining everything that flying is so much about. You know what I mean – all that subconscious pilot fantasy of being encapsulated in your own space-time warp, totally disassociated from real-world anxieties ... or something like that.

So right now, there's no question that the door needs a proper closing. This is not a first. Surely there must be some time-proven procedure to do this in flight. But whatever the cure, it's totally outside my realm of gossip, knowledge or experience.

Keep in mind, closing an airplane door is not like slamming a car door shut. This Bonanza door takes two hands. The door handle/latching mechanism is on the forward (hinge-edge) of the door. The arm rest in the middle of the door is used to pull (slam) the door shut. The slamming and latching operation is done simultaneously, one hand each.

I slow down to 70 mph, about 10 mph above stall speed. Again, no-latch-ability. This is starting to look like I will have to fully stop the plane for a moment or two.

Stopping a plane in flight is not something we do every day. Even though I'm starting to anticipate the opportunity this event might offer, it still deserves a little planning and forethought.

To bring the plane to a full stop here at altitude, I'll have to reduce the power to zero and bring the nose up to a fairly vertical position. There will be a second or two as forward momentum goes to zero and the plane free-falls as gravity starts pulling the weight of the nose straight down.

I wonder if it's unusual that, except for practicing spins, I have never executed a complete, sure 'nuff, fall-from-the-sky *stall*. For all of my re-currency check rides, flight instructors have considered the *approach* to a stall, with the stall warning horn blasting away, and the wings just starting to buffet, to be sufficient.

Since I have plenty of altitude this morning, I decide to execute *my first full, just-fall-from-the-sky* stall. The only risk, then, is that at the exact moment of the nose of the plane falls forward, I will have to let go of the controls *with both hands;*

one to slam the trailing edge of the door and hold it in place, while the other one reaches forward to the leading edge to twist the handle to latch and lock it. This may not be perfect, but it becomes the plan.

It's a clear morning, and I check my six o'clock for any other airplanes sharing the neighborhood. We're all alone. With no small sense of anticipation, I begin the maneuver.

So as not to shock-cool the engine, I ease the throttle back slowly. Then, whilst faithfully holding my 7500-foot altitude, I gradually lift the nose to slow things down smoothly. The angle of attack of the nose increases, and the speed decreases accordingly. All this is comfortably within the bounds of all pilot's familiarity. Then starts the annoying clarion call of the stall warning horn. The ingrained normal reaction for the pilot to hit the power and push the nose over to pick up speed is surprisingly hard to resist. The cockpit gets quieter as the wings start to tremble with the first stage of a stall. It gets even quieter.

But keep in mind, the door in question is in the direct prop blast. This is located exactly where we now want the lowest wind velocity. Any engine power at all is doubly counterproductive. Again, to be certain that this thing is going to work on the first try, it must be a *complete power-off stall and with zero prop blast.* We'll figure out the recovery program after the door is secured. Seventy-five hundred feet is an abundance of altitude. We're a mile and a half high.

The slowing-down process is taking a good deal longer than I expected. In order to reach over to the locking-latch at the leading edge of the door, I have to loosen my seat belt generously. The stall warning horn continues executing its vital duty. Just as the last little bit of lift from the wings drops to zero, the nose of the plane falls like the rope that has been holding us at altitude just broke. I go weightless and release my left hand from the control wheel and right hand from the throttle. We all fall together weightlessly. As I levitate out of my seat and against my loosened seatbelt, my right hand reaches over and pulls the closing handle on the middle of the door – the trailing edge snugs firmly into its jamb. There is no binding. My left hand reaches forward to the leading edge of the door and latches and locks the door handle in place. Snap! Click! These two movements do not take two seconds.

The nose of the plane is now pointing almost straight down and my head is into the headliner of the cockpit. The panorama through the windshield is a rotating National Geographic landscape view of agricultural Georgia at its fertile finest. Without acting like I'm in a hurry, I grab the control wheel, push it farther forward to put some wind over the wings. Simultaneously, I start to ease in a little power. These are deliberate moves but not hurried. The nose drops deeper below the horizon than I want, and the airspeed increases much faster than I expected. Then the stall warning horn clicks off. Because we're accelerating so fast now, I quickly pull the throttle back off completely, and we dish-out from the bottom of the recovery exactly as we're supposed to. Nothing got even a little bit out of whack. Then I cinch up my seatbelt and slow my heart rate down to normal highway speed.

Now, years later, with the privilege of looking back over this whole little event, if I asked myself if it's a good idea to stall an airplane just to close a door, I think I would answer, "With a passenger on board, absolutely not. But if you're by yourself, probably not."

I know – I know. A touch-and-go at a neighborly airport doesn't sound nearly as exciting as falling out of the sky. But some things you can never be certain of until you try.

That's just the way life works. Think about your first French kiss. Same thing. It's no big deal. You try it and it either works out, or it doesn't.

With respect to other unexpected door openings, they are not always so inelegantly handled as the foregoing one. Ten years earlier, as a truly fledgling pilot, I flew my Cessna 172 from Atlanta to Washington, DC and landed at Washington National Airport (now called Reagan International). Upon leaving the airport, the DCA Tower lined me up on what is now Runway 15 and cleared me for takeoff. As I brought the throttle up to full power, WHAP! WHAP! WHAP! I was at 60 miles per hour and just starting to rotate the plane for takeoff when the little aluminum inspection trapdoor on the top of the nose cowling (the one you open to check the oil level in the engine) popped open and started flapping in the prop blast. It startled me so bad that I yanked the power off, slammed on the brakes and stopped right there on the center line of their huge runway. Since the *parking* brake on that old plane had never worked, I had to shut the engine down completely so it wouldn't taxi away from me, jumped out the pilot door, ran around to the engine cowling, resecured the two wing nuts on the inspection door, ran back around and jumped back in, slammed the cabin door shut, restarted the motor, pushed in full power, and headed on down the rest of the runway and into the air like nothing untoward had ever occurred.

The tower must have been watching. As soon as I started climbing out, they called on the radio and asked what that was all about. I answered, "Cessna four, seven, echo. I needed to stop and shut a door. Everything's okay now. Over." This was followed by fifteen seconds of radio silence. That's a lifetime in aviation radio communications. In my mind, I was thinking maybe the Control Tower Operator was talking to the Tower Boss, who was talking to the Head of FAA, who in turn was talking to President Johnson over there across the Potomac in the White House. I wondered if I would have to turn myself in to The Authorities. Maybe now they were even going to take back my takeoff clearance forever!

I was now over the middle of the Potomac River and headed south. This was another one of those moments filled with both guilt and suspense.

The controller then called back and simply said, "Roger." Nothing more. Out of fear of further conversation, I didn't reply.

I continued trucking on down the river and as I passed it, snapped off a crisp Airborne military salute to Mount Vernon sitting there so stately with its lush, green lawn flowing proudly down to the river-edge. What a proud and dignified symbol of freedom in a truly extraordinary country it is.

"God bless America, land that I love."

CHAPTER 8

Schrödingers' Flip-Flop

I HAVE NEVER HEARD of NASCAR inviting regular folks to enter the family SUV in high-performance competition. Similarly, hedge-fund investing is seldom recommended for regular guys working their tails off to keep food on the family table. And believe it or not, performing aerobatics in work-a-day airplanes is sometimes looked upon by some people as *incautious* at best. In other words, there's no reasonable disagreement with the idea that in the orderly world we live in, everything has its appropriate time, place, function, and format.

Universal acceptance of this traditional doctrine notwithstanding, I feel absolutely no shame in stating that I sometimes test the hands-on execution of its practice. Case in point – over the last thirty-five years, I have raced a street-legal 300SL Mercedes, an Austin Healey 100-4 and a Triumph TR-4 in competition at racetracks all over the Southeast. On Sunday afternoons after the last race, and the winners still waiting for their trophies, I'd still be in the pits faithfully putting the windshield back on my car, hooking-up my trailer and exchanging the race tires for street

15 of the 16 Dumbest Things I Have Ever Done in an Airplane

tires. As happy-as-a-pig-in-poop, I'd then drive my race car home. Sometimes I even got lucky and won a trophy.

This proclivity to expand boundaries does not make one unique. In fact, it probably validates normality. Deep down, something like this is what everyone wants to do. Taking this logic another step further, and to prove my point, it follows that anyone who reads a book with a title like the one in your hands right now, will have already stretched an established boundary or two. Right?

I thought so.

Everybody knows that curiosity is the essential fuel that powers the inquisitive mind. Consequently, I submit that there breathes not a person (nor soars not a pilot) who has not found the impulse to overstep that *curiosity temptation* at least a time or two. It might be finger-plucking a major-key interpretation of Beethoven's "Great Fugue in G-Minor" on a ukulele, or it could be in the back seat at a drive-in movie with the windows all fogged up. Either way, exploring boundaries is the foundation of human intelligence. And besides that, TE Lawrence (of Arabia) said, "It is written."

My first airplane was a musty-smelling Cessna 172 that I bought in June 1965 for $5500. I did not yet have a pilot's license, but I knew where I was going. Riveted on that Cessna's instrument panel was a small placard that read: NO AEROBATIC MANEUVERS. For a long time, I gave this admonition little thought. Still, it was a warning that I had to evaluate every time I climbed in or out of the airplane. It was also a constant reminder of imposed limitations. But if you think about it in logical terms, like Newton's third law of motion, this constraint started to make some sense.

As Sir Isaac couched it, "For every action, there is an equal and opposite reaction." Hence, for any action placarded on an aircraft instrument panel, one must expect an equal and opposite reaction to balance things out. And if you don't believe me, just ask Sir Isaac. I'm just a messenger.

Judiciously, my reaction to the placard would have to wait until I had mastered at least a modicum of aviation competence. Maybe I'm just a cautious learner, but it took a couple hundred hours of takeoffs and landings and dozens of cross-country excursions for me to feel reasonably comfortable with most of the fundamentals of everyday powered flight. Eventually, however, that admonition concerning *aerobatics* finally did rear its curious head.

My first wake-up call came one morning when I was flying alone over North Georgia and nobody was looking. Sir Isaac channeled me with the simplest of aviation's forbidden sins. He whispered in my ear, *"Ye knowest the drill, young man. Now craft ye a loop."*

Those adolescent years spent building and flying model airplanes finally paid off. Intuitively, I knew that a loop mostly requires momentum to execute. It didn't take but one high school science class to understand how mass x velocity = momentum. And that momentum is the prime ingredient to executing this maneuver. Even a paper airplane can do loops! So, for my first attempt to loop a real airplane, I started at 7000 feet and pushed the Cessna nose over until the airspeed indicator needle met the yellow caution mark. The instant it touched; I pulled back on the control wheel authoritatively. It was almost in my lap. I held it there and kept my eyes sideways on the horizon just off the left wingtip. The world started revolving around that horizontal axis. The nose of the plane came up briskly, then approaching the vertical we started to lose airspeed rapidly. As we got to the top of the loop, now completely upside down, we continued to slow even more. I became light in the seat, and pulled harder back-pressure on the control wheel, hard enough to at least keep my butt planted. The upside-down part didn't last long – but it was plenty long enough for me. The rapid, downhill (and upside down) acceleration then took over. Being a little overcautious, I held the back pressure a bit too long. This caused the maneuver to end at a higher altitude than where we started. Plus, we were now dangerously slow – just above stall speed.

Holding back pressure too long turned what should have been a nice O-shaped loop into a capital P. It would take another three or four more loops (a week later) before I could relax enough to let the inertia of the plane participate in the zooming-down on the backside of the O. Eventually, I learned to let the plane participate more and more in every phase of the maneuver. The loops got bigger, slower, rounder and, finally, damn near natural. It became just a matter of timing. This maneuver was not conducted by the second hand on a wristwatch. It was timed more by feel and letting the plane do the work.

I could never see the "roundness" of a loop by looking at the horizon off the wing tip. Roundness was more of a sense of butt-pressure, timing, engine sounds, and altitude readings. Changes in airspeed also figure in here somewhere. When you're actually doing the flying, all these mood-swings of airspeed, centrifugal force and wind sounds are self-evident. Explaining it here is like trying to explain sex. You can talk all you want, but you just gotta be there to fully understand what it's all about.

My second airplane was a Mooney Super 21. It looped okay, but it never felt quite as relaxed as the Cessna. Consequently, over time, the Mooney-loop lost a little of its luster. But that's when serendipity opened the door of happenstance.

My buddy Pat Epps and I were flying back to Atlanta from somewhere in his Bonanza. To him, aerobatics is second nature.

His air show routines all over the country are always flowing, graceful, swooping, and twirling. No matter what music is played over the blaring sound system at the air show, I always think of an Epps's routine as executed in a waltz cadence. You know – graceful pauses preceding lyrical flourishes. It's more fluid than gymnastic. Envision a series of arabesques in Swan Lake.

Anyway, he and I were flying along and I asked him about *barrel-rolling* an airplane. Without hesitation, he turned the controls over to me and said, "Here, you take it. I'll talk you through." He narrated and I complied. It was a smooth maneuver and didn't take ten seconds. Done!

Incidentally, his plane was also fully certified for aerobatics. It had quick-release door hinges and everything else required – except parachutes.

A couple of weeks after his talk-through roll, I flew my Mooney up to North Georgia just to bore some holes in the sky. Remember, of course, like the Cessna, this plane was placarded against aerobatics. And you already know what was going on the back of my mind.

It was early Saturday afternoon. The sky was totally uncluttered except for one extremely bright overhead light source about 93 million miles away. To give myself plenty of room to play, I took my time to buy a little extra altitude. At 9000 feet, I leveled off, then banked left and right to look behind me, checking to be sure I wasn't sharing this piece of sky with anybody else. The arena was absolutely empty.

I dialed the RPMs up to 2,500 and brought the throttle up to full power. Then I eased the nose over to bring the airspeed needle up to the caution line. This is the same opening exercise you do for a loop. Just as the needle touched the yellow caution mark, I pulled the control wheel back to bring the nose up level to the horizon. At that point, I cranked the control wheel all the way over to the right – to the stop. As the left wing got up to the vertical, the nose started dropping down below the horizon. I knew *in that instant* that my entry to this roll was way too flat. In the next second and a half, I was going almost straight down – inverted – at full power.

This was very bad.

The nose continued to fall even faster till there was nothing in the windshield but lots of that incredible virgin forest that blankets the Appalachian Mountains.

In one motion, I pulled the engine power full-off and hauled back hard on the yoke. This felt like the backside of a loop, except I was going too fast. The airspeed indicator needle continued up past redline. As the plane started pulling out of the inverted dive, centrifugal force pulled my glasses off my nose and they vanished somewhere. My blood went from brain to toenail, and my peripheral vision started losing color. In only a couple of more seconds, the plane finally started flattening out, but the airspeed was still way above the red – NEVER EXCEED – line on the indicator. I was also going in the opposite direction from whence I started! I had dropped vertically nearly 5000 feet –call it a mile– in just a few seconds.

I haven't mentioned this next consideration because it wasn't important until just now. At the beginning of this flight, curled up in the copilot seat beside me, was my trusty old dog, Luke. He's a loving, semi-bright, brownish, mix-breed mutt I got from the local pound for $25. He got his name from the movie I now call *Cool Paw Luke*. I invited him to come with me this morning as a test dummy. His sole purpose was to evaluate my first perfect *solo roll*.

If I had executed this maneuver flawlessly, he would have snoozed there, oblivious to all things going on around him. The balance mechanism in his ears would only sense a slight increase in gravity (actually centrifugal force) and maybe some wind-noise aberrations. Consequently, I had expected his continued tranquility would render silent testimony to the incredible flying skill of his master, Moi!

However, when the roll started going sour, his body slammed straight up (actually, down) into the headliner of the cockpit. Then, somehow, he ended up on the floor and under the rudder pedals on *my* side of the plane. After I finally recovered from the failed maneuver and had gotten everything else under control, I tried to coax him out from his new found haven of security. There was no way he was coming out to the light of day. In fact, I couldn't even get enough leverage to drag him out roughshod, i.e., fistfuls of skin and fur. He and I had to fly back to Peachtree Airport with him wide-eyed and cowering under the rudder pedals. Keep in mind, aircraft rudder pedals are also brake pedals. Consequently, we then had to land without using much of either lest I squeeze the juices out of poor 'ole, frightened-eyed Luke.

Once the plane was parked, I crawled in under the control wheel to haul him out more gingerly than my previous in-flight efforts. The story that dog's eyes told me after he was finally in my arms cannot be expressed in anything so flimsy as the written word. But whatever it was, it went straight from his trusting, pure-beating canine heart to my guilt-ridden, imperfect human soul. After I secured the plane in its tie-down spot on the tarmac, he and I drove directly over to Pat Epps's house.

Pat listened patiently to my description of the failed maneuver. Then, rocking back knowingly in his lawn chair, he said (in his best senior-pilot voice), "Come by Peachtree tomorrow afternoon, about four o'clock, and I'll take you up in my plane and teach you how to fly. And don't bring the dog."

I was at his office at four and flew left seat (pilot's seat) in his certified aerobatic airplane for an hour. Pat never touched the controls. Man, what a difference it makes flying a truly maneuverable airplane with somebody who knows what they're doing.

In this lesson, there was never a feeling of either mystery or danger. He just talked to me like he was showing me which way he wanted me to mow his lawn. No hurry. No scorn. No bombast. No superiority. Just two guys transferring information. And just like the micro-DC current that runs our brain waves, it was all flowing one way.

The lesson was not just numbers and physics. It was more like a psychology class. Sure, numbers always count. But for true aerobatics, your relationship with the plane must be based on something a little bit removed from hard science. The pilot must feel the exact-same acceleration, momentum, and centrifugal forces that the plane feels. Only then can harmony be established.

Over the following decades of our friendship, Pat and I will fly side by side in cockpits ranging from a fifty-year-old Douglas DC-3 Gooney Bird to a modern business jet. But even when I'm pilot-in-command, he will always be the senior pilot – the one I will forever look up to with unwavering respect and admiration.

Eventually, both rolls and loops became a comfortable part of my aviation vocabulary. However, on one long, 1,700-mile *solo* cross-country flight from Winnipeg, Manitoba, back to Atlanta in my Mooney, my aerobatic urges started percolating. I wondered how many rolls I could link in a row. Maybe after you get the rhythm, it can be done indefinitely. But, as it turned out, that doesn't work for me.

I was flying along in the great unpopulated middle-belly of Canada and connected eight aileron rolls together like linked sausages in one continuous air-screw maneuver. At roll eight, "motion-uncertainty of balance and stomach" became the limiting factor. For the rest of that very long day, I was treated to one of Mother Nature's more unsavory lessons in the consequence of inner-ear balance disorder.

Years later, however, on another long, uneventful flight, I was flying along in an endless cloud bank on solid instruments to pick up my wife, Nancy in a little town in Tennessee. This was in 1982 in my Bonanza. Air Traffic Control assigned me an altitude offering zero visibility and zero turbulence. Conditions were really boring and I got to thinking. *Since I'm just sitting here doing only what FAA tells me to do, I wonder if it's possible to roll an airplane without any outside visual reference of any kind.* Giving it a little more thought, I also wondered if a pilot can actually "feel" a roll. *Maybe I should first try one with my eyes closed. The maneuver doesn't take but seven or eight seconds.* The thesis of my failed test with Luke in the Mooney suggested that one cannot feel a well-executed barrel roll. *Yes. I screwed up that one with him, but I'm more experienced now and in a more maneuverable airplane. I wonder...*

So, *can it be done?* The answer, of course, is, *certainly*. But clearly, the intelligent way to execute this stunt is to start on a clear day with good visibility and time each phase of a roll with a stopwatch, and quantify the angle of each pitch of the nose. Then write it all down so you don't forget it. But I haven't done any of that. And currently, I've gotten my head all into this idea of doing this thing 'cause I'm bored.

There are also a couple of other practical considerations that might deter aerobatic maneuvers on instruments. One is that airplanes flying *on instruments* are monitored by FAA radar. However, their radar receivers (in those days) only show aircraft locations and do not show their *altitude*. Consequently, airplanes flying under FAA scrutiny, must have a separate *altitude* transmitter working in harmony with their radar transponder to send all this good information to their radar station. [8] This permits them to keep everybody separated both vertically and horizontally.

As I'm flying along right now, just toying with all these random notions, I can't shake the fundamental idea that a roll-in-the-blind must be a worthy endeavor. And it might even add a little something to the dimension of instrument flying. Maybe it's all part of that process of the inquisitive mind expanding its boundaries we touched on earlier. Or maybe it's just more of that Sir Isaac mischief. Who knows?

The bottom line is that this whole notion is simply one of those things in life that you either do it or you don't. If you don't do it, nobody knows anything about it. If you decide to do it, very few people will understand the motivation it took to exercise such a stunt. Consequently, what difference does it make whether you do it or don't?

Without giving it any more thought one way or the other, I continue sitting here unemotionally watching all the instruments in front of my nose stay faithfully inert exactly where they are supposed to stay.

But just then, right there on the right edge of my field of vision, I see a hand reach out and turn off the altitude transmitter on the transponder. This is a starter's flag if I ever saw one. In conditioned response, I push the nose of the plane over to pick up speed. Visibility outside the airplane, of course, is still zero. When the airspeed needle dials up to the yellow-caution, you know the drill by now. I pull back on the control wheel and hold it

---

[8] In those days.

till I think the nose must be about 30 degrees above the horizon. Without question, these first few seconds of this maneuver are the most important in this whole exercise. The new angle of the nose will determine the vertical profile of our invisible inverted trajectory!

To lessen the opportunity of repeating my too-flat entry in my flubbed roll with Luke, today I bring the nose of the plane up to what I feel is a shade higher than where I would normally put it. This might add one more second of timing. I don't have a stopwatch, so I just squeeze my brain for one additional second. I then rotate the control wheel to the right until it comes hard against its stop, and start a count: "Hut thousand, two thousand, three thousand, four thousand." [9] At this point, I should now be about upside down. Of course, I still *feel* right-side up. I hold it another half-second and release the slightest amount of pressure on the ailerons. I don't know why I do that, but I always do. Maybe it's simply a memory reflex of a bad habit. But for me, it just feels familiar.

Completely inverted and with a quick scan of the instrument panel, everything's all centered like nothing is going on. I think this is good. The altimeter shows us 200 feet above our Air Traffic Control assigned altitude. That's not perfect, but it still feels within bounds. The engine sounds good. It's *not* overrevving and the slip stream sounds about right. The airspeed indicator shows us slowing a little, but still within bounds. Completely inverted and too slow would be very serious.

I have to trust that I am now completely upside down. I push the controls a tad forward to keep the nose from dropping. My weight in the seat feels about normal – maybe a little light, but still okay. We keep on rolling (I think). So far, nothing untoward

---

[9] This is the same count we used in the 82nd Airborne Division when jumping out of C-119 Flying Boxcars back in 1954.

has happened. I count another four thousand, and I should be all tucked-in, right-side up (Oh, man. I hope I am). The magnetic compass says we are still on course, and I can see that we're a hundred feet above our assigned altitude. I give the instruments (and myself) a few more seconds to slow down. I cannot express how much I want to know if we are in level flight or not. After less than 20 seconds of this search for validation, I watch the familiar arm (still wearing my blue shirt) just reach out and switch the altitude transmitter back on. Still cautiously, I enjoy the furtive satisfaction of thinking that I have gotten away with something that absolutely nobody – including me – ever saw happen. *There are no witnesses.* And except for these brief words that I'm writing right now, it is totally unrecorded history.

Now think about the case of Schrödinger's cat at altitude. If this morning's event were not observed, then this roll did not actually happen.[10]

Still sitting here with nothing else to do but steer and hold altitude, I again have time to wonder what the hell brought on this stunt. My long-view guess is it was simply an incautious but necessary challenge to broaden certain undefined personal limitations.

But that's such a doopy statement that it probably doesn't mean anything to anybody but me. And even I am unsure of it.

On the other hand, there is no question that experiments of this nature are not for everyone. For a few, however, this, or something like this, might simply be how the tempos in the Code of Life are played. And everybody's tempo is different. Some us march to it – some run and some dance to it. And some might just smile, tap their toe and not really get involved.

---

[10] Schrödinger posited that if one put a cat, plus something that could kill the cat (a radioactive atom), in a box and sealed it, one would not know if the cat was dead or alive until the box was opened. Consequently, until that time, the cat was both dead and alive – or neither.

Schrödingers' Flip-Flop

And if this last option is chosen, might I not then persuade such a soul to ask of themself, "Might I enjoy rolling an aircraft while fully blindfolded with only the musical cadence of my harmonica for a time reference?" Well, of course, no one should try it. But if they did, while sucking and blowing the "Battle Hymn of the Republic," the maneuver would be finished just as they get to, "Where the grapes of wrath are stored."

CHAPTER 9

Taildragger

IT'S JUNE 16, 1988, and I'm up to my ears getting loose ends lined up for the Greenland Expedition Society's fourth endeavor to the ice cap. Our departure date is this coming Tuesday, June 21st. In all the chaos going on right now, the only diversion I look forward to is that I need to get checked out in a *taildragger* before we depart.

A taildragger is the airman's scorney epithet for an airplane that has its third wheel at the tail end of the fuselage. Most modern airplanes have that third wheel of the tripod up under the nose. This is called *tricycle* or *conventional* landing gear. In the olden days, before airplanes had electric starters, the low tail and high nose made some sense. It put the propeller of the plane high enough for somebody to be able to pull *down* on it to hand-prop (start) the motor. One of the big drawbacks of having the nose that high, however, was that it made it difficult for the pilot to see the runway over the nose while taxiing. Someone then figured out that if the tailwheel were moved up under the nose (thus leveling the airplane), several other good things happened. First, the pilot would be able to look straight ahead when flaring to land. Second, the taxiing operation became more like driving a car – meaning you could actually see where you're going. And the third benefit was that when taildraggers brake too hard (or stop too quickly), they would sometimes tip up on their nose and screw up the propeller. The nose wheel eliminated these adverse conditions.

Pat Epps's Taildragger with retractable skis

For use on our expedition in 1986, Pat Epps, my partner in the Greenland Expedition Society (GES), bought a Cessna 185 with retractable skis. As with most ski-planes, it was a taildragger.

Responding to the fundamental difference in the landing characteristics between conventional and tail-wheel aircraft, FAA requires a pilot to be checked-out in tail-wheel aircraft before its use. Because I had never been checked out in an airplane of this configuration, I didn't get to fly it. Three takeoffs and landings with a flight instructor remedies this issue. No big deal.

CW Marlow is the executive director for GES and will serve as my check pilot this morning. He's a well-qualified aviator with lots of taildragger time. We have flown together enough that we're both respectful with the other guy's flying experience.

This morning's check ride, of course, will be in Pat's Cessna. Next week, he and I will fly it up to the Greenland ice cap to continue our quest to retrieve the Lost Squadron that crash-landed there in 1942. The eight planes in that group now languish there some 250 feet deep in the glacier. So how do we get them out from that much ice? Addressing that question is why we're going up there.

After we finish my check ride this morning, Epps Aviation's Maintenance Department is scheduled to reinstall the retractable skis on the plane. We will then be able to land on regular paved runways, grass strips and, finally, on the ice cap.

In terms of my flying experience, I have more than 3,000 hours as PIC and hold instrument/commercial/multi-engine ratings. I'm also checked out in corporate jets and sailplanes. Although my aerobatic experience is fundamentally homespun, it is not inconsiderable. With all these hard-earned credentials, I look at the check ride this morning as mostly a matter of subscribing to FAA rules and protocol.

This morning, CW and I will fly straight from PDK over to Lawrenceville Airport. It's less than a twenty-minute flight. I'll make two takeoffs and landings there, and then we'll fly back to PDK for the required third one. After that, we both go back to work. This should not take much more than an hour out of each of our busy schedules. Besides, it ought to be fun.

In preparation for today's ride, we have spent not one minute of our time sharing any of the technicalities or characteristics of taildragger flight (or landing) operation. CW assumes that I'll just do it. More importantly, I know damn well I will.

Another support of the positive notion of things, is that in the last year I've flown over to the Lawrenceville airport a half dozen times in my Bonanza to practice and perfect short-field landings. The Bonanza handbook declares 1,450 feet to be the minimum distance for landing that plane over a 50-foot obstacle. At the Lawrenceville airport, the distance from the runway threshold to the first turnoff from the runway to a taxiway is 1,200 feet. Performance standards for aircraft manuals are established by test pilots and set high targets for us everyday pilots to shoot for. Because I practice it frequently and I ignore the 50-foot thing, I usually beat the Bonanza's certified minimum landing distance by 100 feet or more. The weather this morning is perfect for precision landings, and I'm absolutely confident of my skills. No. I have never flown a taildragger before, but hey ... an airplane's an airplane. Right? Just remember: "When the trees get bigger, you just pull back." What more do you need to know? (That's supposed to be cocky mirth.)

After pre-flighting the Cessna, CW and I hop in. I know the starting drill, and we head out. He's in the right seat. The takeoff from PDK is by the book. The power settings are pretty much the same as my plane. The airspeed is a little slower, but all in all, this is a familiar flight.

The downwind and base legs at Lawrenceville are at the same altitude, distance and airspeed that I'm accustomed to. Except for the fact that I don't have to lower the landing gear on this plane, the final approach feels completely familiar. There is no wind to compensate for. I slow the plane to 75 knots as we turn onto the final approach to the runway.

While descending down the invisible glide path to the runway, my air speed and altitude stay spot-on. Coming up on the runway numbers at the threshold, we're at exactly 60 knots and only four feet above the ground. This approach could not be more accurately flown. I pull the throttle back to full-off. With 30 degrees of flaps, we immediately settle into the cushiness of ground effect. Oh, man. This feels so exactly right!

It's so familiar that in a flash decision, I elect to give CW the *Full Monty* of extreme aviation excellence. I am going to make the first turnoff from the runway at 1,200 feet! (The Cessna spec sheet calls for 1,400 feet minimum landing distance). The two main-gear tires touch down exactly where I want them to – right at the two-foot point of the approach stripes. As I would in my airplane, I'm immediately hard on the brakes. Simultaneously, I ease back on the yoke to bring the tail wheel down so I'll have something to steer the tail end of this thing.

The tail comes down, a little stronger than I expected, and not exactly centered behind the main landing gear. It's off to the left a little bit. I brake both wheels hard, but add more pressure to the left brake to straighten us out. The tail then swings hard to the right – but it keeps going on around in front of us in a 180-degree arc! I'm now locking up both brakes, and the plane leans over. The right wing-tip scrapes the runway hard as it arcs around. The tire-screech lasts not two seconds. The plane stops completely, right on the centerline of the runway, but cocked up on the right main landing gear. Then it rights itself proudly on both main gear and one tail wheel. Everything is quiet and still. The engine is still idling over patiently, but we are facing exactly in the direction from whence we have just come.

The good news is that I landed and stopped in less than 300 feet! Other than a complete crash landing, that might be a record.

I look over to CW and say, "Oops!"

He looks at me quizzically. "Well, what the hell did you do that for?"

"I don't know. I was trying to make the first turnoff. These planes are supposed to land-short, aren't they?"

"Well, sure. But you got to learn to land them first."

Let me make this clear. Underneath this artificial humor, I just made an incredibly big, dumb, very expensive, stupid-ass mistake. And let there also be no question that one's own unabashed, ego-driven blunders are the most onerous ones to swallow. You gag on them. It's easy to scoff and dismiss other people's errors. But when it is so completely yours – and so obviously the product of high-strutting false pride and unadulterated ego – it changes you. I mean, it changes you to the core. Fortunately, this lesson in false humility never goes away. *And, I memorialize it here in the written word so that I may continue to feel its value (shame) for the rest of my natural life.* But the good news is, the chances of my repeating this one blunder becomes pretty slim. But if it does happen, it will be the product of something other than unabashed-ego and flaming-bravado.

But right now, I need to leave this crime scene and find a telephone to tell Pat that I just wrecked his airplane.

I give the engine a little throttle and steer us off the runway to a taxiway and then park behind a nearby hangar and shut the engine down. This area of the airport looks devoid of human activity. I'm starting to wonder if maybe my egregious little *faux pas* may have gone unnoticed.

CW and I climb out of the plane and walk around it to assess damage. Right off, there are a couple of big disappointments. First, the right wing-spar is noticeably bent up from the wing strut (the diagonal brace) attachment point. The tip of the wing is eight or ten inches higher than the other one. Second, the right horizontal stabilizer is also bent up about five inches. Both the right aileron and right elevator look pretty buggered up. I leave CW to keep checking things on the plane while I hustle around to find a phone booth.

"Klondike? We got a problem. I just ground-looped the Cessna."

"Hmm. You bend the prop?" (Notice that he doesn't ask if anybody got hurt.)

"No. The prop's alright, but we bent the wing spar and the horizontal stabilizer."

"Will it fly?"

"Yeah, sure, probably."

"Good. Then bring it on back over here, and we'll fix it up." There is no tone of admonishment in this conversation. Obviously, he has no idea how insufferably overstuffed with confidence my head was only twenty minutes ago.

"All right. We'll see you in a little bit."

When I get back to the plane, CW is still poking around and assessing damage. I tell him, "Pat said if it will fly, to fly it back."

With that, CW stops what he's doing, looks at me straight in the eye and says, "Really?"

"Yeah. But we still oughta look at things just to be sure."

He goes back to his inspection of the plane, not talking. I can feel his heavy-thinking impulses from twenty feet away. When he reaches into the cockpit and operates the control wheel to check the ailerons for movement, the right one is binding metal to metal with the wing. I go over to it and twist and wiggle everything to help it work. It looks like it's just the aileron skin scraping against the aluminum wing surface. With my pocketknife, I carve the aluminum wing-skin back half an inch to where it's not rubbing and works freely. I then push and pull the wing tip up and down vigorously to test to see that it is still securely attached to the fuselage. There is no suggestion of loose movement. It feels solid.

The horizontal stabilizer is even easier. I just step up on top of it and bounce gingerly. It goes back into position (as well as one can judge by eye). The moveable elevator works freely without binding or conflict.

I tell CW, "Okay, man. Lez go."

CW is conspicuously uncommunicative right now. But as we all know; quiet recalcitrance can sometimes speak volumes. Obviously, he's still uncomfortable with our field repairs. He looks me straight in the eye.

"Richard, I think I'll fly."

I offer no argument. He climbs into the left seat. I take the dunce seat next to him.

To maintain level flight in a straight line, CW must fly with the control wheel rotated about 15 degrees to the right. Other than that, the short trip back to PDK is uneventful. He makes a flawless landing (show off!) and taxis over to Epps's maintenance hangar. Pat comes down from his office with a cadence of a Prophet descending a Mount. He looks at the plane and, with a crooked smile, says, "You know, I'm not sure I would have flown this plane back here."

For the next few days, the Epps's mechanics work on the airframe almost around the clock. A bent wing spar is no small task to repair. When the work's finished, Pat test-flies it and declares it okay. Then I take it up again. This time I go with a sure-enough certified taildragger flight instructor. My log book notes nine takeoffs and landings in the two-and-a-half-hour session. All maneuvers and landings are acceptable. A few of them are even pretty good.

There is no showing off this time. That old Mr. All-Full-of-Himself is now the new Mr. Humbler-Than-Thou, thank you.

My Log Book will include many more taildragger flights and landings, some of them in big taildragger airplanes like the Douglas DC-3. But I am never again confident that I am the master of this arcane landing event. I will become proficient in the technique, but not in the natural art. Every future landing in a taildragger will be at full concentration from the beginning of the approach to turning off onto a taxiway. And only then will I cautiously transition from an intense flying mode into a relaxed taxi mode.

Oh. One more thing. Somebody did call the authorities to report my ground loop. Five months later, to maintain my commercial license, the FAA required that I take a flight proficiency check-ride with a highly qualified FAA Check Pilot. The flight test was straightforward and in my own plane. Not a taildragger. I passed it with an easy margin. It was a serious but pleasant morning ride, with an exceptionally well-qualified pilot. I told him in great detail and absolute honesty exactly what happened with my errant ground loop. He responded with the old story line about the relative size of pilots' heads and their britches.

His comment was neither officious nor condescending. He also said something about *overreaching* being a thing all pilots do at one time or another. *"Hell, that's what your first solo was, wasn't it?"* His words.

Besides, how else, other than overstepping some known boundaries, can one ever "slip the surly bonds of earth, and touch the face of God"[11]?

---

[11] High Flight, John Gillespie Magee

CHAPTER 10

The Iceman Cometh

ORDINARILY, ONE DOESN'T think of a stray cloud in a blue sky as a clarion call to arms. But I can remember, as a young pilot, looking up and seeing a wandering cumulonimbus passing overhead, and I could hardly wait to get to the airport. I just wanted a piece of that fluff!

Now, as an old pilot, I may still glance at a gray, overcast sky and recall a specific flight that my memory bank has filed away only for occasional personal indulgence.

Kindly permit me to share one such event that took place in my Mooney on November 30, 1974.

Nancy, now six months pregnant with our first child, is in the right seat. We had just spent a gracious Thanksgiving holiday visiting her family down in Bryan, Texas. On the way back home to Atlanta, we stopped to spend a night with good friends in Greenwood, Mississippi. The weather for the next (and last) leg to Atlanta is forecast as overcast (clouds) with bases at 1500 feet and 3 miles visibility. Legally, this is still visual flight rules (VFR), but for a couple of hour trip, it's a little dicey. To make things easy for my passenger(s) and me, I file an instrument flight plan. This will get us above the cloud layer for an easy, clear ride all the way home. The top of the cloud layer is forecast at 6000 feet.

We depart Greenwood at 0900 and climb right through the overcast to 7,000 feet into the clear air. The weather may be a little gray and gloomy above and below us, but hey, at least we're *not* in the soup.

I mentioned that Nancy is pregnant. But even if it doesn't show yet, there is something there that ties us together in a new and invisible, steel-forged way. She's still tall, brown-eyed, shapely and exceptionally beautiful. Her temperament is still reserved and controlled. Whatever this new bond is, we're both fully appreciative of it. It's as welcomed as it is precious.

Okay, back to flying.

We're approaching the Georgia State Line – less than 45 minutes to Atlanta. Atlanta Center radio relays a Pilot Report to all planes in the area. A Beechcraft Baron, 30 miles west-northwest of Atlanta, reported moderate icing at 3,000 feet. This area is uncomfortably close to the approach route we plan to use to get into Peachtree Airport, (PDK).

This is not good. Besides, I'm not sure what *moderate icing* means exactly. I suspect it to be something *more than a light* but less than *a heavy* ice buildup. I would rather know if it is *rime ice* or *clear ice*. Rime ice is usually a frosty nuisance. Clear ice is dense, like an ice cube. Whatever it is, I have virtually no experience with any kind of icing. But currently, since we are now being dealt the *ice-card*, there is nothing to do but learn how to play it.

A common perception of an aircraft "icing up" is that the weight of the ice brings the plane down. The truth of the matter is, ice is far more insidious than that. It's not the weight that kills. It's the *icy deformation* of the wing and propeller profiles that causes the *loss of lift* of the wings and the *loss of thrust* of the propeller. Weight simply exacerbates the issue.

A few minutes after their ice-warning call, ATL Center hands us off to ATL Approach Control. Approach will sequence us to line up for the landing procedure at Peachtree Airport. They direct us to descend to 3,000 feet. I radio a request to them to permit us to maintain our 7,000-foot altitude until we are lined up on the instrument approach. My thinking is that this will keep us clear from picking up any ice (of any nature) until we are descending on the glide slope down to the airport. This will put us in the potential icing conditions for only three or four minutes. Inasmuch as ice can accumulate only in a visibly-moist environment (clouds for rime ice, or rain/drizzle for clear ice), once we're below the clouds, there will be no more opportunity for either type of frosty accumulation. Besides, by then, we'll have the airport in sight. In a nutshell, my game plan is to minimize our duration in the clouds to just a few minutes. And even that brief time will be on a downhill slide into the clear air beneath the ice-danger zone.

Approach Control, however, denies my request. They radio back that because of their traffic load, we must get in line behind two airplanes in front of us and follow the standard landing procedure just like everybody else. This also means flying through the same clouds that iced the Baron. My guess is that this procedure may take twenty or thirty minutes. It could be longer.

I don't like this plan and haven't answered Approach Control. They repeat their instruction for us to leave our clear-air altitude and descend into the ice-producing clouds below us. They also give us headings to swing north and away from PDK to start our full approach procedure. Eventually, they will turn us around to get in line for the instrument approach behind the planes ahead of us. It looks to me that this full procedure will definitely put us in the ice-making clouds for even a more extended period than I speculated. I can't speak for the other pilots in line, but I don't like this situation one bit. Then again, maybe this icing thing won't be as bad as it sounds. Who knows?

Obediently, I descend down into the cloud-layer below us. Immediately, ice starts to accumulate on the windshield. At first, it's not very thick, but it eventually covers the windshield from the engine cowling up to the top of the windscreen. And it's not the frosty rime-ice stuff either. It's the real McCoy – clear ice! Forward visibility then steadily diminishes to zilch. This took only a few minutes.

Atlanta Approach Control is still running the show. Between the big Atlanta Hartsfield International Airport and PDK out here in the burbs, Approach has a dozen or more airplanes they're playing with. I have only one. And right now, my one is having an issue. I make another radio call.

"Atlanta Approach. Money two-eight-yankee. Request direct heading to PDK, and clear us for a descent to 2000 feet." The elevation of the airport is 1000 feet above sea level. They're calling their ceiling at 1500 feet. Consequently, the cloud layer is 2500 feet above sea level. My request will put us 500 feet below the ice-making moisture layer. Again: if there is no visible source of moisture, there will be no icing.

They reply, "Atlanta Approach. Negative on the heading and altitude change. We can only line you up for the ILS approach. You're now number two in line."

Again, this full-procedure can still take twenty more minutes. We have no control over how far Approach will take us out before turning us back for the final approach. That also goes for the plane in front of us.

The windshield ice continues accumulating. It's now too opaque to determine its thickness. Forward visibility no longer exists. The cabin is notably darker. I check the altimeter. We're level at 3,000 feet above sea level. As I pointed out, the base of the cloud layer is only 500 feet below us. I look out the side window and watch the wing accumulating more ice. But I also catch glimpses of thin areas in the clouds behind the trailing edge of the wing. Then I make out fleeting pieces of tree-covered *Georgia* below! Then, unexpectedly, there is a fissure in the clouds. I see the intersection of Interstate 85 and Atlanta's I-285 Perimeter Highway. This is Spaghetti Junction and it's only 3-miles from Peachtree Airport! In that instant, I drop the left wing and dive directly through the opening in the clouds.

The moment I am below the overcast, I'm in clear air and legal for visual flying. I no longer need an instrument approach. I immediately call ATL Approach, tell them I'm visual and to cancel my instrument flight plan. They acknowledge so quickly that I feel they are glad to get rid of me. I then call PDK Control Tower. "Peachtree Tower, Mooney, one-nine-two-eight-yankee, VFR, three miles northeast, landing Peachtree with information Echo."

Because it's too crummy a day for any kind of casual flying, there is no other visual traffic in the airport pattern. And because all the other planes landing here are on the icy approach to the instrument runway, Tower immediately clears us for a visual approach to their secondary runway, Runway 27. This is the airport's shortest runway and is ordinarily used for smaller and slower traffic like Piper Cubs. The long runway, like the one we just abandoned with the instrument approach, is used for business jets and faster aircraft on instrument approaches.

What a huge relief to get out of the icing conditions. My big problem now is that the windshield is still completely iced over.

15 of the 16 Dumbest Things I Have Ever Done in an Airplane

It is opaque. The plane's wings are also iced from the leading edge back about three feet. Obviously, there is absolutely no way of knowing what this ice is doing to our stall speed. Normal stall speed for the Mooney is 58 miles per hour. Since the lifting capacity of our wings is already enormously compromised, I arbitrarily pick 100 miles per hour as the minimum airspeed I will maintain. I resolve not to fly any slower than that speed until we are over the threshold of the runway and able to flair for a landing.

Landing at nearly twice the stall speed is called *landing hot*. But it's possible. Stalling out with an iced-up wing at low altitude is called *deadly*. It's frequently unrecoverable. I'm good with *hot*.

While I'm thinking all of this through, the engine suddenly starts vibrating wildly. My first thought is that it broke a connecting rod. In one motion, I pull the power back but have to push the nose over to maintain my 100 mph. An immediate instrument scan shows no loss in oil pressure or any unusual engine overheating problem. The shaking must be caused by ice on the propeller blades. Only one blade has lost its ice and thrown everything out of balance. If so, that's both good and bad. Good because now, we have at least one clean propeller blade pulling us, and bad because it could shake the engine out of its mounts. There is still zero-forward-visibility through the windshield. Looking out the side windows is good. I can see the profile of Atlanta's high-rise skyline 15 miles to the south of us.

Of course, the tower cannot see any of our issues and clears us to land on their short, 3,400-foot crosswind runway. This runway is about half the length of the instrument runway. I would be happy to share my overall ice plight with the tower and request the long runway, except the shorter runway is right under my wing. With all the engine shaking going on, I need to land this airplane as quickly as possible, not as soon as somebody else thinks it fits their schedule. Running off the end of the short runway is survivable. I maintain my rapid descent with my airspeed faithfully pegged at 100 miles per hour.

When I turn left to line up on runway 27, we're higher than I want to be but still holding our speed. I lower the landing gear and start pumping in full flaps. Because I still cannot see straight ahead, I drop the left wing, cut the power back to idle, push the nose over to hold my speed and slip sideways, straight for the big 27 painted on the end of the runway. The sideslip provides a reasonable view of the runway through the side window. With no engine power, the propeller vibration is minimalized. I'm burning off altitude about as fast as it can be done while still holding our aggressive descent. As we pass over the big 27, we're only ten feet above the runway, but we're still going 100 mph. I lift the nose a tad to start slowing things down. We're coming into ground effect – that most welcome air cushion under the wings that won't go away until the wheels touch down.

To straighten the plane out enough to fit on the runway, I ease off the rudder to let the nose line up where I can sense the center line of the runway should be. With no forward visibility, I keep my eyes on the runway lights off the left wing. This works well. We continue to float along for an agonizingly long time. Maybe 100 mph was too high a number. Maybe it only needed to be 75. Too late now for second guessing. The wheels are now less than two feet above the runway. The power stays full-off. We're decelerating very slowly. I can't wait, so I reach over and retract the landing flaps back to zero.

This causes the nose to pitch up a few degrees and the wings to lose some lift. The plane drops that last couple of feet with a firm *thwump*. Hard braking then brings us down to taxiing speed – say, 15 miles per hour. There is still almost 200 feet of unused runway ahead of us. We continue slowing to its end, then turn

15 of the 16 Dumbest Things I Have Ever Done in an Airplane

right onto the last taxiway. I radio, "Peachtree Tower, two-eight-yankee taxiing to Epps tie-down."

After I park the plane in our home tie-down spot, unload everything and tie down the wings, I ask Nancy to come up to the nose of the plane to look at the big chrome spinner at the center of the propeller. It has an 8 inch long, 2½-inch diameter ice stump projecting exactly straight ahead. It looks like a 20-mm cannon sticking out of the nose-spinner of a World War II Bell King Cobra. It's about the dimensions of a very large ear of corn. I break it off at the spinner to take home to store in the freezer. (Naturally, it melted to a wet spot on the floorboard of my car before we got there.)

On that drive home, Nancy and I don't talk about this icing incident at all. There really isn't much to discuss. A situation came up. I made judgments about complying *and not complying* with ATC directions. I broke out of line when I thought I could see a large enough space below the cloud base that I could escape flying through more icing conditions. Was that a good call? Neither of the other planes that stayed in the system crashed. But maybe they had deicing equipment, equipment that I do not have. I don't know. But I do know this. I acted when I thought I needed to, and we're driving home this afternoon. And we're not talking about it.

A few days later, however, Nancy does bring it up. She fully understood everything that was going on. We're finishing dinner now and she opens the conversation with something about how dangerous that whole situation was. She does not criticize any judgment I made, nor does she lay down any new laws I have to follow in the future. She simply states, "Richard, I'm not going to go through that experience again. On any future flight we make, if there is any reasonable chance of icing, I'm asking you to tell me. I will make my own judgment as to whether I go with you, fly commercially, or cancel my trip." She pauses, then adds, "And, just so you know, I will probably fly commercially."

And that's it. No bellyaching, no crying the blues and no hard positions of control. No nothing except that she is not going to go through this experience again. Her position in shared risk just established boundaries. Not particularly boundaries for me. It is for her personal option to make her own choices. This kind of thinking is not for everybody, but for us, it works. I completely welcome her decision.

In the ensuing decades of our marriage, we will raise three children. There will be only one time when she and the kids will fly commercially while I solo home in the rain. It had nothing to do with ice. It had to do with "a chance of embedded tornados." Nancy said that this condition fell into the "chance of icing" category. That was good enough for me. Our taxi dropped the family off at the commercial gate at Pensacola International Airport and me at the General Aviation terminal. Late that evening, when we all finally regrouped at home in Atlanta, the kids were still excited. All I heard was, "Oh, Daddy. The airplane was so big you could stand up in it! And it had these big seats and they brought us things to eat and we could talk and …"

Prior to that flight, the kids had never flown in the quiet comfort of a commercial airliner. Never in my life could I have imagined that I would ever have to listen to a kid whine, "Do we always have to take Daddy's airplane?"

CHAPTER 11

"Roll The Pole"

ON AUGUST 12, 1980, Pat Epps and I flew his single-engine, aerobatic, Bonanza from Peachtree Airport in Atlanta to the Magnetic North Pole. It took three days to get there and four days to return home. The Magnetic North Pole, of course, is not like its static and responsible big brother, the Geographic North Pole. The Geo-Pole is a fixed spot in the Arctic Ocean around which our Earth spins. Sure, it wobbles around a little bit from stuff going on in the belly of our planet, but in general it stays pretty close to its proper axis. The Mag-Pole, on the other hand, is an inveterate rover. In 1980, it was moving around the Arctic Ocean along the north edge of Canada's Arctic islands. The Geo-North Pole was another 500 miles farther north.[12] Yes, the difference between the two poles has been a source of navigational gymnastics ever since the magnetic compass was first used in China back in the eleventh century AD.

As one might expect, this whole notion of flying to the Magnetic North Pole was birthed sorta out of wedlock.

---
[12] Of course, it was north. It's north of everything on earth!

15 of the 16 Dumbest Things I Have Ever Done in an Airplane

To wit: In August, 1978, Pat, Zip Martin and I were attending the world-famous Oshkosh Airshow in Wisconsin. We flew up there in Zip's Bonanza and landed midmorning with plenty of oomph and bounce. The scale and energy of all events-aviation was, for us, what you might call, overwhelming.

By the end of the day, we three ended up mostly horizontal in the pleasure of the shade under the low wing of the airplane. It was time for us to check out the survival gear I had packed before we left the Sunny South. It was safely stored in a big blue-plastic ice cooler. The peak heat of the afternoon had passed and the grass in the massive aircraft parking area smelled freshly mowed. There was also the gentle background whining of somebody trying to get in one more loopty-loop routine. I can't speak for my two buddies here, but for me, this special moment of reward was slipping into one of those spiritual things that sometimes generate otherworldly notions. Hence, almost like it had waited for us, a novel notion joined us.

It started with Zip. Out of nowhere, he pipes up, "Okay, guys. So now that we've done Oshkosh, what are we going to do next?"

Of course, this is bazaar-talk. We had not seen even a quarter of what there is to see here. I was sure that Zip felt it too, but he was of no mind to let prudence, protocol or moderation interfere with the designs of the crazy-notion-whims.

Nonetheless, the gauntlet was thrown. Pat was stretched out in the grass with his head propped against the right landing gear tire. Thinking that he was asleep, I took on the bait. Naturally, I tried to answer the screwball question with matched, screwball cleverness. "Well, since we're already a third of the way there, why don't we just keep truckin' and check out the North Pole?"

Pat, without removing the vendor's brochure folded over his eyes, immediately piped up and said somewhat authoritatively, "No. I wanna go to Narsarsuaq."

"Roll The Pole"

Narsarsuaq is a small village near the most southerly tip of Greenland. He was referencing a trip we three, plus our friend Mike Pickett, had taken the previous year. On that occasion, we flew Epps's Piper Aztec from Atlanta to its new owner in Birmingham, England. We four rotated taking the pilot's seat. Pat was flying the long overwater leg from Canada to Narsarsuaq, Greenland. By the time we approached their airport, the weather had turned lousy. I was in the seat behind Pat and, leaning over his shoulder, showed him a way for us to go back out over the Atlantic Ocean and come in below the low overcast. I then showed him how we could fly up a broad fjord to the airport, land safely and refuel. He didn't buy my plan, but kept looking down for breaks in the undercast. We kept circling above the airport two more times. There were no flaws in the cloud cover, so he announced, "We're going on to Kulusuk." Kulusuk is 480 miles north of Narsarsuaq.

We eventually landed there, but I never let his judgment-call stand in the way of my ragging him about his dangerous and wussy decision (that somehow worked out so well).

Okay. That's history. It's now a year later and we're back at the airshow in Oshkosh.

As we were relaxing under the wing of the plane, even though the theatrical effect of the North Pole idea was now spent, I can't exactly explain why, but I kept promoting it. I think that the greatest merit of this destination was its obvious improbability. Who do you know ever went to the North Pole on a whim?

By chance, we had 2 aviation charts that extended to the Arctic Ocean. They offered enough info for us to calculate the 500-mile distance between the two Poles.

Interestingly, however, the location of the *Magnetic North* Pole, as it appeared on our charts, lay just off the north coast of the Canadian Archipelago. But it was still in the Arctic Ocean. It also appeared that if we could get to the town of Resolute Bay on the Northwest Passage, the Mag-Pole might be just within the fuel range of the Bonanza. It was starting to look like maybe this screwball adventure might be possible!

Then out of the blue, Pat amended his preferences. "Hell. Either Pole's fine with me. You guys figure it out. I just want you to know that I'm coming back by way of Narsarsuaq."

Well, there it is. The Program Concept Phase is complete. We're going to the Magnetic North Pole!

Now it was time to develop a Planning Phase Program:

- Arctic gear – none
- Emergency food – none (but we do carry a nice survival cooler that is about to need restocking)
- Canadian/Arctic navigation charts – a few
- Life jackets and raft – neither
- Emergency radio transmitter – none
- Survival gear/rifle/ammo, etc. – none
- Funding – well ... None of us carried credit cards in those days. Since we were using Zip's plane, Pat and I were buying the gas for this Oshkosh trip. I had some cash in my wallet – maybe a hundred and fifty bucks. Pat had some cash. I don't know how much. Zip always carries a big roll of dough. We are all too macho to ask each other how much cash he carried. So, hell, we'll leave costs unresolved until we run out of money.

So that's it. The Detailed Planning Phase is now complete. We'll simply have to figure out the rest of whatever we need to know as we go along.

After we crab-crawled out from under Zip's plane, we bummed a ride in a pickup truck into Oshkosh, got a room in a modest hotel, and had a splendid dinner in an upscale restaurant with linen tablecloths and fresh flowers. Sun-up the next morning we caught a taxi back to the airport, checked the weather, loaded up in the plane, and took off northbound to the Magnetic North Pole.

I flew the first leg to Thunder Bay, Canada with Zip as copilot. The weather was postcard perfect all the way. Piece 'o cake.

Zip flew the second leg to Big Trout Lake with Pat in the right seat, and Pat flew the third with me as copilot; destination: Churchill. This is a fair-sized township on the west coast of the mighty Hudson Bay. The folks up there should be able to outfit us with all the stuff we'll need – food, warm clothes, a gun and some ammo, and most importantly, some real information about where we're going.

The densely wooded midriff of Canada is huge. We had just started our search for the Hudson Bay somewhere out in the middle of the endless wilderness when, suddenly, the plane's engine started making angry growling noises. From the back seat, Zip said, "Don't worry about it. It always does that when you get too far away from civilization."

Epps and I, being more cautious by nature, didn't buy that pitch. Without peer discussion, Pat did a gentle 180 and pointed the nose of the plane south toward the United States. I spent my time looking for crash-landing sites, adjusting engine power, fuel mixture and RPM settings to minimize the grinding, knocking, grunting noise. The oil pressure and engine temp stayed normal. The clatter did not get worse. Other than no small amount of personal tension, we made it back nearly 400 miles to Thunder Bay on Lake Superior without any problems. The weather was clear all the way and the landing a most welcome event.

When we discovered that there were no aircraft mechanics at the airport to help us evaluate our problem, Pat and I started removing cowlings and inspection plates to look for evidence of any oil hemorrhage or physical discord. We found nothing out of order. Since Chicago was only three hours down the west shoreline of Lake Michigan, we decided to stretch our luck one more hop. This would, at least, get us into US territory.

We landed at Midway Airport in downtown Windy City under a full moon. ATL was only another four hours away. The engine noise sounded no worse than when it started this morning. Besides, we were now so used to it, we could hardly hear it. You already know what we did next.

At midnight, somewhere in Kentucky, we had to navigate through a line of thunderstorms embedded in a cold front. This flight was an unbelievably bad call on our part. Decisions of this nature are sometimes characterized as *stupid*. That it turned out well doesn't upgrade the characterization of our choice – not even a little bit.

After worrying our way through this ferocious and particularly ugly weather-front in the middle of the night, the green and white blinking light of Peachtree Airport came up star-lit and welcome under our nose. It was 1:30 in the morning. We found out the next day that the engine chatter was a failing muffler baffle. This is not a big problem until the baffle breaks off and clogs up the system's exhaust flow. In that case, the engine may well choke to a stop. But that didn't happen.

Isn't it curious how, when you look back on circumstances like this, you see things so differently? In this situation, our tempting Fate with such blatant disregard for consequences and our immature optimism yielded absolutely no appropriate consequence.

In terms of judgement calls. We got a failing grade.

In terms of borrowed luck, we got more than our share.

One year later, in 1979, both Pat and Zip expressed absolute *zero interest* whatsoever in going north again to find the Magnetic

North Pole. Zip said, "Hell no, Richard. Didn't you get the message? We got a free pass last year. I know when to rest on laurels."

Apparently, it was only I who had touched the Tar Baby. So, on August 10th, I got in my old Mooney, put food, Cokes and a sleeping bag in the back seat, a bundle of money in my pocket and headed north – *solamente*. Inwardly, I smiled, thinking that my good buddies back there in Atlanta would soon regret their wussy-overcaution.

The weather was rotten-assed the entire way from Georgia to the Hudson Bay. It took two long, hard days just to get to Churchill. After leaving there, I stopped for fuel at a mosquito-infested place called Baker Lake. The mosquito density in the Arctic can be magnitudes greater than in the Okefenokee Swamp. In the swamp, you smack individual offenders. In the Arctic, you have to wipe them off like army ants.

From Baker Lake, I headed up across the Arctic Circle and into what turned out to be impenetrable Arctic weather. I was so determined in my cause, that I set good sense aside and flew into the frosty muck anyway. Of course, there were no electronic navigation aids anywhere up there where I was exploring. Satellite navigation was more than a decade in the future. The radio-direction finder in the Mooney had stopped working a couple of days earlier. The magnetic compass was beginning to wander aimlessly and the sky was always far too overcast to shoot sun-compass readings.

Flying blind without even the suggestion of visual or electronic navigation aids became the background dirge for serious soul searching. As I write it here, all the reasons to just turn around and fly home sound simple and logical. But when you're doing it, logic sometimes loses its grip. The emotional voices in my head were rhythmically chanting, "Keep going. Keep Going. Don't turn back!"

The logical side of my personal mindset responded by setting time limits and counting minutes and seconds as each change in plan was made.

When it's nut-cutting time, there is no limit to all the scenarios that you can juggle in your head.

"If I can't get a sun-fix in ten minutes, I'll ..."

"If I don't pick up a radio beacon in twenty minutes, I'll ..."

"If I can't get a visual fix in five minutes. I'll ..."

"If the mag compass doesn't respond in ten minutes. I'll ..."

My airspeed was 155 miles per hour. The problem was, it was in some unknown direction against (or with) unknown Arctic winds. As I said, there was no radio or navigation connection with anyone. One might think, "just follow your compass." Well, I'm still hundreds of miles from the Mag Pole and the compass has already started its errant behavior. It works dutifully for a while, but then takes a brief wandering excursion. Without either shooting the sun, or tracking something on the ground, or receiving electronic bearings, there is no way to find the magnetic pole – or even which way you're going. There were times that I estimated that I didn't know within 200 miles where I was – except wherever it was, the weather was shitty.

On the other hand, it did not take any fancy instruments to tell me that it was also as lonely as lonely gets up here.

Then the engine sputtered. *That's okay, I expected it.* I had purposefully run the left fuel tank completely dry. I had been flying for two-and-a-half hours. Total fuel exhaustion would be in approximately 150 more minutes. The idea of running the first tank dry is that when the other tank, the one that is now full, starts sputtering, I don't spend any time or attention trying to squeeze a little bit of juice out of a *nearly empty* tank. When I'm out of gas, I'm out. No more distractions or multitasking. I will spend all my time and energy focused on one thing – making my first off-airport, dead-stick landing… and it better be good!

"Roll The Pole"

A couple of hours ago, when I took off on this last leg north, I pledged to myself that if I ever got to the halfway point *on fuel* and did not have a rock-solid connection with my next destination, I would turn back.

Well, this was it. Half my fuel was now gone and I had no idea where I was.

Now let the cower-home-phase begin!

A quick thought flashed through my mind, *If I got here with a tailwind, I'll not make it back to where I started.*

I switched fuel tanks and the engine fired back to life. Still flying on solid instruments in opaque cloud, I did a timed 180-degree reversal in course and then hoped to heaven that I could find my way back to Churchill. My best shot to find it was to head southeast and find the Hudson Bay. This is the largest inland body of water in the world. Traditionally, the weather over a body of water will differ from the weather over the adjacent land mass. If this happens today, I could then visually follow its western coastline south to Churchill. That might not sound like much to hang your hat on, but right then it was all I had.

But it worked. An hour later I picked up the Churchill radio beacon and gave them a call. They replied that their airport was at instrument weather minimums, and forecast to worsen. At that point, that airport would be closed to all traffic.

As it happened, everything worked out nicely. All the worry was for naught. I eased right on in, tied the plane down, thoroughly enjoyed a rather lonesome dinner, and decided that it was time to retire from all this folly. I spent the night in a boarding house type facility and the next day started the long flight home. Maybe this was cowardice on my part. But it made no difference. There simply were not enough positive vibes going on in my head for me to keep pressing on. This battle was over.

I lost.

The next three days were spent wimping 2000 miles back to Atlanta. Thankfully, 90 percent of the weather on the way back home continued to be terrible. If it had been pretty, I would have felt even greater humiliation. With my tail between my legs, I eventually tied-down the Mooney at my spot at PDK.

I remember reading somewhere that, "Of all sad words of tongue or pen, The saddest are: 'It might have been.'"

But I must add something else here. It was not the superficial words of failure that hurt. It was something much more visceral, something deep in the gut. My only grain of salvation was that I knew damn good and well that I would return. Of that, there was no question.

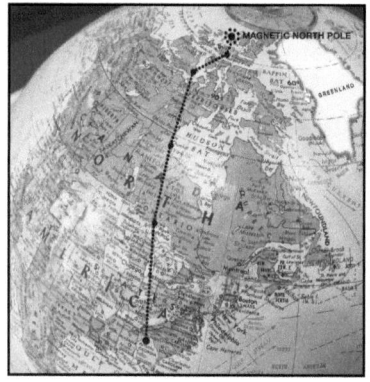 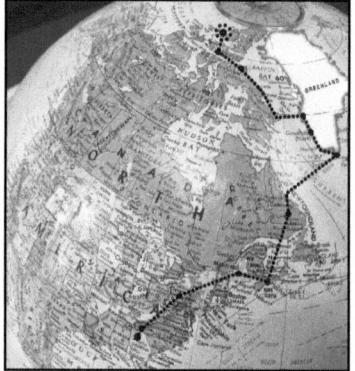

To the North to the Pole, 1980   Return from Pole, 1980

That was 1979. It's now 1980. Of course, I told Pat all about last year's failure. I believe he enjoyed it. Can you believe that? Without provocation, he then had his maintenance guys put a 15-gallon fuel tank in the back seat of his Bonanza and said, "Come on, Super. Lemme show you how to do this thing."

"Roll The Pole"

We then flew from Atlanta right up to Resolute Bay in the prettiest weather ever witnessed in North America. Well, maybe that's a little exaggerated because Pat did have to make a zero-zero landing at Resolute. *And it really was 0-0!* After the plane rolled to a stop on the gravel runway, we had to just sit in the cockpit for half an hour until the fog lifted enough that we could finally see an airport fence. We then cranked up the engine and taxied to the gas pumps.

Obviously, this is Pat's story to tell, not mine. But if you ask him, I'll tell you right now what he'll say: "Aw, it wasn't that big a deal. You just pay attention and do what you're supposed to be doing, and everything'll all work out just fine."

After we finally found the airport terminal and checked in at the Quonset hut hotel, we had a most pleasant dinner with some local pilots. I believe we were looked upon as something of a curiosity.

The next morning broke with a scattered-to-broken cloud cover. We took off early and headed north for the final execution of this venture – to *roll the Magnetic North Pole!*

This time, we had warm clothes, MREs (military Meals Ready to Eat), life jackets, a life raft and a 12 gauge with slugs to keep errant polar bears at bay. And, of course, we also had our trusty blue survival cooler. Man, this felt good.

This was August 12, 1980. The weather was mostly scattered clouds; certainly not bad enough to hold off our final run.

At a hundred miles out from the Pole, the magnetic compass was wandering way off course. More often than not, it simply stopped rotating altogether. At about 50 miles from our destination, it became inert. It was locked on 330 degrees. Our altitude was 7500 feet. The scattered cloud layer below us looked to be about 3500 feet above a sprinkling of tundra islands. The sky above was a deep royal blue. The shapes of the islands easily matched-up to our aviation charts. Visual navigation was a snap. We needed neither compass nor solar shots. The vastness of the Arctic Ocean a few miles up ahead carried an array of broken ice flows. We navigated by both following islands on the chart and sun shots[13]. Keep in mind that the Magnetic Pole is not a precise point on the surface of the globe like the True Geographic Pole.

It's a geographic *region* some miles in diameter. Also, don't forget that it is also always moving. A short study of the nature of the North and South *Magnetic* Poles suggests that they completely reverse themselves four or five times per million years. For a four-and-a-half-billion-year-old planet, that's a whole lot of flip-flopping going on.

We were still 20 or 30 miles out from the centroid of the Mag Pole region when I suggested to Pat, "Klondike. I haven't rolled this plane in a couple of years. Whatcha think about my doing a practice one out here?"

"Naw. Practice when we get there. Just don't screw up."

Made sense to me.

Ten minutes later, having reached our destination with the full horizon of the Arctic Ocean ahead of us and with no further fanfare, *one of us took the controls and became the first pilot to ever Roll the Pole!* Then the other guy took the controls, did a 180, and was the first pilot to ever *Unroll the Pole*. That second guy then rolled it a second time to also hold the title of having the most Rolls of the Pole in recorded history. The two guys then

---

[13] For a sun compass, we used a pencil as a vertical sundial gnomon and let its shadow cast on a hand-drawn circle with 360 degrees of marks at 10-degree increments. To set the shadow, we multiply Greenwich Mean Time by fifteen (the number of minutes it takes for the sun to travel one degree). We then subtracted our estimated latitude. Then we took the reciprocal of that number to calculate the shadow, put the shadow on that final number, and the 360-degree compass card is oriented to Geographic North.

shook hands and took a Sacred Arctic Oath to never tell anyone who did what that morning.

Now, to answer the big question, "What did the magnetic compass do at the Magnetic Pole?" The answer is simple. The compass in this Bonanza clung steadily to 330 degrees. If you flew this way or that way or upside down, it stayed locked on 330°.

Think about this. The direction of the magnetic flux (flow of energy) *at the Pole* is exactly vertical to the Earth below. There is no horizontal component to give it any parallel-to-the-Earth directionality that the rest of the world is used to. Also, an airplane has a small magnetic field of its own. It creates what is called *magnetic deviation* on the compass in the airplane. When the Earth's horizontal magnetic attraction goes to zero, as it does at the Poles, there is no Earth-born horizontal force for a horizontal compass needle to respond to – except for one thing: *–that small magnetic field of the airplane.* This is demonstrated by the fact that all aircraft magnetic compasses have a *deviation card* right under the instrument. This card quantifies how much deflection the magnetic field *of that particular airplane* makes to its aircraft compass reading. Airplanes are regularly checked to update these changes in its magnetic distortion. The procedure is called *swinging the compass.* I've done this a number of times on my own plane. In fact, it's kind of fun to taxi out to the airport's *compass rose* to quantify your own plane's magnetic field.

It was now time to head home. Of course, we returned via Greenland and stopped at Narsarsuaq. Pat made the landing and was finally cleansed of all sin!

But let me remind the world of this: No one has ever rolled the South Magnetic Pole. You up for it? Chicken if you don't!

Taylor and Epps just truckin' on home

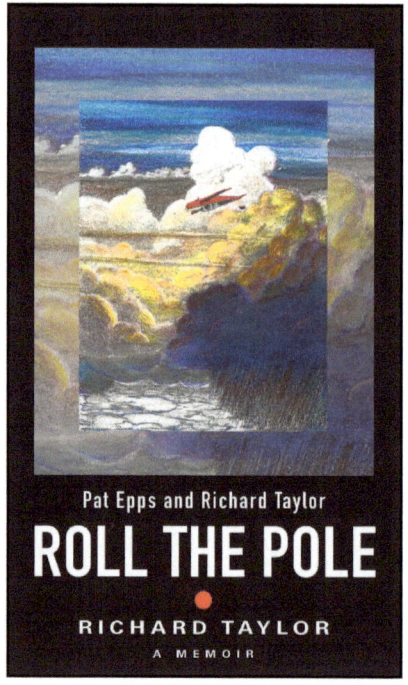

For a more in-depth description of this adventure, visit:
https://www.amazon.com/gp/product/0998752819/

CHAPTER 12

"Glacier Girl"

IN THE SUMMER of 1942, on their way to The War in Europe, a squadron of eight US Army warplanes ran out of fuel and bellied in on the Greenland ice cap. The flight consisted of two Boeing B-17 "Flying Fortress" bombers and six Lockheed P-38 "Lightning" fighter planes. Two weeks later, all twenty-five chilly but thankful airmen were rescued by a US Coast Guard Cutter, *Northland*. No one was left behind. All of the men were given two weeks R & R and then sent back to the Front. The war ended three years later, and the airships were left where they lay. Eventually, they got covered with snow and ice and became known as the Lost Squadron.

Thirty-nine years after that, in 1981, Pat Epps, of Epps Aviation fame, met a guy named Russell Rajani. Rajani told Epps that he held the Rights of Search and Salvage for the Lost Squadron. Sensing a unique opportunity, Pat called me up on the phone, and we set up a meeting for the next day with both Rajani and his partner, Roy Degan. They had created an aviation adventure company called Pursuits Unlimited (PU). Just to keep things balanced, Pat and I registered an LLC[14] that we named the Greenland Expedition Society (GES). Pat was president and I was VP and treasurer. The two corporations then made a joint venture agreement to salvage the Lost Squadron. The agreement provided that PU was to provide the Rights to the ownership of the planes. GES's responsibility was to locate the planes on the ice cap and then return them to the US. At that point, the two corporations would each take half-ownership of them. Sounds simple enough, doesn't it?

Since all four of us were pilots, occasionally, at a few moments of whim and fancy, we also toyed with the idea of flying the planes off the ice cap and right back here to Georgia – wing-tip to wing-tip. Hmm.

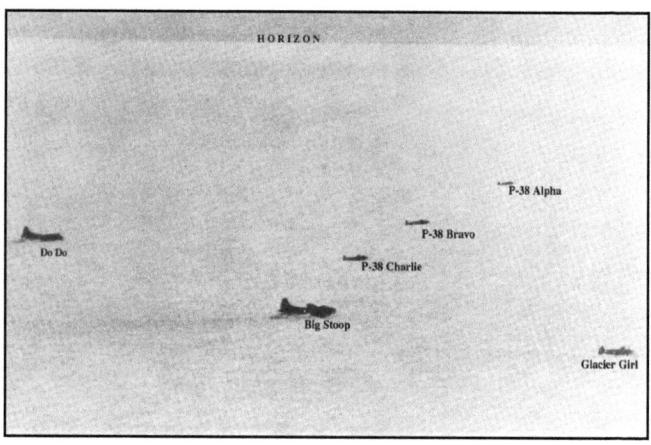

Six of the Lost Squadron. July 1942

---

[14] Limited Liability Corporation

"Glacier Girl"

Glacier Girl, 1942

But first things first. First, we had to find the planes and asses their condition.

Step one: In August 1981, the four of us took off from Atlanta and flew to Greenland in a four-seat Piper Aztec we borrowed from Pat's brother, Doug Epps. Our mission was to pinpoint the location of the planes, assess their condition and decide in what manner they should be returned to the States. Flying at least a few of them back was becoming an increasingly attractive fantasy.

After camping out on the ice cap for three days, we located not a single piece of evidence of the existence of any of the aircraft. To make things worse, the metal detectors we took with us also detected absolutely zero sign of anything made by man there or in the general vicinity of the coordinates of the landing site.

Obviously, this first sortie to Greenland ended up as a conspicuous mission failure. On the flip side, however, we did learn a little bit about putting together an arctic expedition. That is to say, we learned how to get up on the ice cap, pitch a tent and prepare a warmish MRE[15] – all without the surface winds of 50 to 75 knots blowing us off the glacier or our simply freezing to death. Don't laugh. Knowing how deep to dig-in a tent and erect

---

[15] Military Meals Ready to Eat

wind-walls and determine the tent entrance weather-orientation is a hellofa lot bigger deal than it sounds. But here's a hint; except by chance, nobody gets it right the first time. However, after that, everybody gets it right.

Let's call this rather expensive failed mission: **Strike One**.

First Camp Site – 1981 Greenland Ice Cap

Our second expedition was a couple of months later, October, 1981. This time we took with us a highly respected geophysicist, Bruce Bevan, PhD. He brought with him his state-of-the-art subsurface, ground-penetrating radar unit (GPR).

We landed in Sondrestrom and chartered a DeHavilland Twin Otter on skis to fly us 350 miles to the Site on the opposite coast of Greenland. Just before the weather on the ice cap turned completely wicked, we did manage to get within a few miles of our destination. The Twotter (Twin Otter) pilots decreed that there was no way to land safely anywhere near the site. Or even if we could land, there was no way for anybody to find us to bring us back. We had no option but to turn back to Sonde.

Whether success or failure, expedition money-clocks keep ticking at their own relentless pace. The first expedition cost us about $15,000. This one was already costing more than twice that. It was embarrassingly painful to return home again so completely empty-handed.
Strike Two.

Our agreement with Rajani expired in December, '81. Rather quickly, however, he landed a deep-pocket sponsor, the R. J. Reynolds Tobacco Company. Reynolds and Rajani then formed the Winston Recovery Team. They put together a formidable expedition in 1983. One of their members later told us that they ran through a quick million dollars. They located the planes on GPR, but concluded that they were buried *very deep* in the glacier and, therefore, *not recoverable*. So they folded up their tents and left.

The next year Epps and I heard that Rajani's couple of subsequent recovery efforts had failed to make any meaningful progress. Their lack of progress kept GES's ears perked.

Since Denmark was still serving as the Protectorate of Greenland, they were the grantor of the Rights of Search and Salvage for anything on the island. In 1983, I contacted the Assistant Minister of Greenland, Sven Adsersen, to ask if the Rights were now available. He knew about our two failed efforts in '81, but stated that until Rajani finished his contract with Denmark, he (Adsersen) was not in any position to talk to anyone else about the Lost Squadron.

A year later, Rajani's contract expired. I called Adsersen again in the fall of 1984. This time, he said he was now open to a conversation about our interest in salvaging the planes. After a few more telephone calls back and forth, I flew to Copenhagen and finalized the negotiations for the Rights to be assigned to the Greenland Expedition Society starting in 1985.

We were now back in the game.

Our third expedition was in 1986. Pat had called Dr. Bevan to come back with us. Again, from Sonde, we chartered a ski-plane and returned to the original coordinates of the site. After almost a week of search, we *did not* find anything except an incredibly beautiful virgin glacier. The cause of our failure to find the planes was attributed to our not bringing the correct crystal-frequency for the Ground Penetration Radar unit to use in ice – or something like that. Whatever our error (or ignorance), this expedition was another failure.

The lesson herein was not about "three strikes and you're out." It was more about Epps and me not having the personal geophysical experience it takes to the lead a technologically sophisticated enterprise as we were undertaking. And just to make this point clear, I'm sitting here pointing my finger at myself.

Strike Three

A Frozen Caldera?

"Glacier Girl"

Pat and I tried about as hard as we could to put together an expedition in '87, but we couldn't make it happen.

As a little personal background, Pat and I both graduated from Georgia Tech. His degree is in civil engineering and mine in architecture. This doesn't mean we're engineering wizzes, but I hope it suggests that we both know how to apply at least some measure of engineering principles to new and technical challenges.

In that light, and after our last failed mission, Pat called the Georgia Tech Geophysical Department and asked them to help us understand the scope of everything we don't know about Arctic geophysical exploration. In response, they invited us to their hidden-away off-campus facility and personally tutored us in some fairly arcane disciplines – including the difference between magnetometers working effectively in the vicinity of the Magnetic North Pole versus the non-magnetic properties of ground penetrating (GPR) systems. We even got into the powerful effects of the extraordinary solar storms that occurred on the surface of the sun while we were out there in the summer of 1981. Of the eleven years we will work on this project, those geophysical lessons still stand out as high points in this adventure. Go, Yellow Jackets!

A successful entrepreneur named Don Brooks, who lived down there in God's Country, (middle Georgia), heard about what we were doing and wanted to be part of it. Not only did he own a DC-3, aka, *a Gooney Bird,* but he was also eager to share its use. Don, who is smarter'n hell anyway, was tireless in his dedication to finding the airplanes. Much of his motivation was fueled by the fact that during World War II, his father was a B-17 tail gunner. Don was also planning to rebuild a B-17 like the one his father crewed. Obviously, he was also interested in collecting as much Flying Fortress paraphernalia as possible. As our relationship

15 of the 16 Dumbest Things I Have Ever Done in an Airplane

matured, his time, energy, generosity, engineering knowledge and unfailing friendship was collectively, one of the greatest assets the GES enjoyed. And if that sounds like a big statement, it is!

Our fourth expedition was in 1988. With the determined efforts of our new geophysicists, Austin Kovacs, we located the planes using his ground penetrating radar *of the correct frequency – 5 MHz*! Then, using the 3.5-inch-in-diameter aluminum nozzle attached to the end of a 260-foot-long high-pressure steam hose, we "thumped" the B-17 bomber, "Big Stoop."[16] Thumping means that the melt head hit something solid. Yes, the *something* was, in fact, very deep in the glacier – 250 feet, to be exact! Although we made good progress that summer, we did not achieve our goal – to physically sit in a Lost Squadron airplane.

Let's call this **Strike Four**.

The next year, 1989, was our fifth expedition. Don built another melting device he called a *thermal meltdown generator* (TMG).

---

[16] Big Stoop was a character in the comic strip *Terry and the Pirates*.

This device was designed to melt a shaft large enough for a person to be lowered down in a harness to the B-17 bomber and return. The melt-head was three feet in diameter and shaped like a very large, rounded kid's dreidel[17]. The plan was for it to melt through the glacier using gravity to guide it straight down. It worked flawlessly for a while. However, when it reached a depth of 70 feet below the surface, it stopped. When we went down the shaft to look at the problem, the TMG was lying in quiet repose on its side on a base layer of solid blue ice. What we discovered was that the composition of the glacier at that depth changed from the porous layers of granular snow between the ice lenses, into a solid, blue foundation of ice that went down another 2,500 feet to solid earth below. We later learned that geologists call the top of this ice layer a *firn line*. The increased density of the glacier negated our concept of the Gopher using *gravity* as a descent-guide. Guiding must be mechanically controlled. Since we didn't have the physical resources to change our guidance system *in situ*, there was nothing to do but pack up and head 3,000 miles back home for more design/build work. Here again, we did not achieve our goal to get into a plane.

Strike Five.

I believe it!

---

[17] A four-sided spinning top, played during the Jewish holiday of Hanukkah

15 of the 16 Dumbest Things I Have Ever Done in an Airplane

As painful as it is to go through each of these operational disappointments, our Arctic experience would occasionally show glimmers of damn-near competence. This positive appellation would later be confirmed when Epps and I were invited to give a presentation of our work to the scientists and faculty of the Richard E. Byrd Institute of Polar Studies at Ohio State University. Their almost-smiling recognition of so many of our mistakes was balanced by embarrassingly generous praise for our not-to-be-minimized achievements. They understood immediately every grief, success, and nuance we shared with them. This unexpected recognition permitted us to see ourselves through a significantly different lens than what we were used to. No, it was not like we were all of a sudden big-shot explorers. It was more like we were warmly welcomed into a quiet fellowship of an incredibly exclusive club.

After our technical presentation to the faculty and scientists, the college organized a large student assembly for us to deliver our more user-friendly version to those who wanted to come. The full-house attendance was gratifying.

Taylor and Epps place Old Glory at B-17 Big Stoop

"Glacier Girl"

The next year, 1990, was our sixth expedition. This time, we teamed up with a highly respected general contractor, Pizzagalli Construction Company from Burlington, Vermont. Angelo Pizzagalli was their head honcho and, as it turned out later, probably the most determined and tireless worker on the cap. Their contracted responsibility to us was to bring at least one complete P-38 Lightning up to the surface.

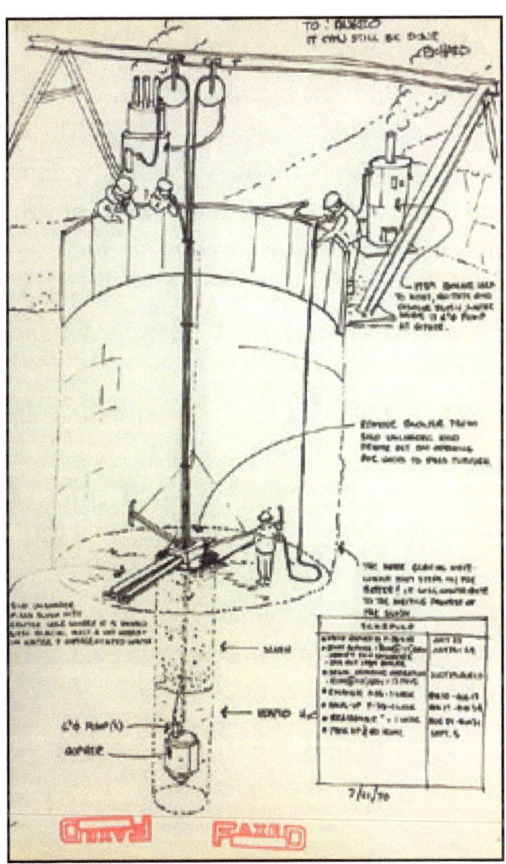

Silo-Unloader Shaft Modification Sketch

Several times, we had forty people working in the excavations. The Pizzagalli Team effort used a physical *ice-grinding* device they developed to core a 16-foot diameter shaft down to a plane. But after it ground its way down 175 feet, the shaft flooded and they were forced to stop. They got down to an incredible 100 feet *below* the firn line (water table).

Simultaneously, the Greenland Expedition Society was *melting* a three-foot diameter shaft 250 feet down to the B-17, Big Stoop. The smaller diameter GES Gopher shaft collected substantially less water and eventually reached the bomber. We found the plane smashed and unsalvageable. The area immediately surrounding it was then melted-out to create a work area large enough for us to scavenge a healthy collection of historical aviation paraphernalia. We hauled out machine guns, the throttle quadrant, cockpit instruments, ammo, combat helmets, the entire upper gun turret, and much more. Some of the engineering efforts from both teams worked out fine, and some didn't. But in the end, we did salvage a handsome array of aircraft parts.

GES's agreement with Pizzagalli expired at the end of the expedition. Since we had finally gotten to sit in a Lost Squadron airplane, Pat and I were now ready to go back to attending to our work-a-day livelihoods and spending time with friends and families. We felt fairly satisfied that we had taken this mission about as far as one could reasonably go.

However, since we *did not* meet our goal of retrieving an airplane: **Strike Six**

Gordon Scott on the B-17 Big Stoop (250 feet deep in Ice Cap)

Then came 1991. A fellow named Roy Shoffner flew his twin-engine Beechcraft Baron into Peachtree Airport and taxied over to Epps Aviation for fuel. He met Pat, who then called me, and new enthusiasms were born. Roy explained that he always wanted a P-38. We came to an agreement for him to be a financial partner for one more Greenland Expedition Society foray.

It took us a full year to put together all of the components for this next expedition. In Don's freshly repainted red DC-3, the GES returned to the site in May 1992. This new mission started with first thumping a P-38 with a probe, then melting a series of four ice shafts in a row with a melt-head Gopher. Each shaft was ±four feet in diameter. We left a ±two-foot web between the holes so they could be dug out by hand. This permitted us to melt and dig simultaneously. Once the webs were removed, we were left with a 4 x 22-foot slot in the glacier – 260 feet deep. This was the minimum opening through which we could lift the wings and the large fuselage center-section to the surface.

Glacier Girl in all her glory, 1992

Neil Estes hauling out Elevator Section

"Glacier Girl"

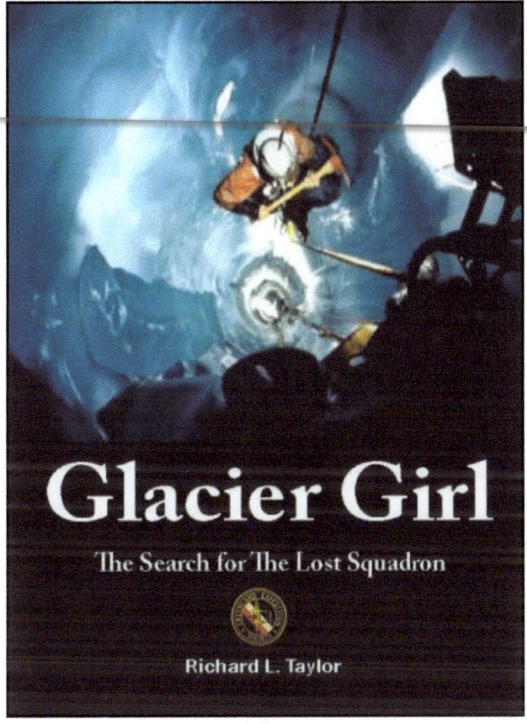

For a more in-depth description of this adventure, visit
https://www.amazon.com/Glacier-Girl-Quest-Richard-Taylor/dp/1663240310/

Concurrent with the melting operation, the P-38 was being carefully deconstructed by skilled aircraft mechanics. As the slot got wider, we could lift the larger pieces of airplane to the surface. Once all of the components were on the surface of the cap, we flew everything to Kulusuk. From there, the large components were then freighted to Sweden where a cargo ship picked them up and delivered them to Savannah, Georgia.

GES agreed that Shoffner would undertake the restoration of the plane. Everything was then trucked to his home town of Middlesboro, Kentucky for a total restoration.

Finally: a **Home Run**.

Graduating Class 1992

However, the personal and economic saga was not yet over. After all the pieces of the plane were back in Atlanta, Pat Epps threw a big Hangar party. It was a party we will all remember.

But soon thereafter, the dollar-dust from the last eleven years of Arctic antics gently settled into an enormous and now identifiable *liability of significant dimensions.* The bottom line, as they say, was that the GES was in "very disappointing financial order."

Probably sensing this, Roy made GES an offer, and the Greenland Expedition Society sold him its half-interest in the recovered P-38 Lightning. Roy then hired our GES Executive Director, Bob Cardin to run the restoration project, and the two of them undertook the task of putting Humpty Dumpty back together again. It took them ten years and, rumor had it, 2-million dollars to put her into like-new flying condition. And what an outstanding job they did! She was once more a raving beauty, and Roy Shoffner named her *Glacier Girl*.

In 2002, from the Middlesboro Airport, she made her first flight in fifty years. It was awe-inspiring. The History Channel featured her in the one-hour special, *The Hunt for the Lost Squadron*. This is an incredibly well-crafted story. Later, Pat and I were asked to make an auditorium presentation at the Air and Space Museum at the Smithsonian in DC. The packed house made it a perfect exclamation mark to put on the end of a long but gratifying adventure.

Glacier Girl *center section* headed to Atlanta

Yes, I know. These seven expeditions over an eleven-year period are not the aviation antics of performing barrel rolls in the blind or flying a plane by shifting body-weight in the back seat.

But it still has plenty of the elements of *derring-do* laced with errors and blunders. It was not scripted. It was frequently treacherous. It was always expensive. We made lots of mistakes. It was compulsive and it was addictive. Plus, there was the requisite evidence of collateral damage to family, friends and business – all the obligatory hallmarks of *daring beyond reason*.

Update:

Glacier Girl is currently (2023) owned by Rod Lewis, president of Lewis Energy Group in San Antonio, Texas. She now flies as a star attraction in airshows all over the country.

Closing Thought:

"Nothing in this world can take the place of persistence.
Talent will not; nothing is more common than unsuccessful men with talent.
Genius will not; unrewarded genius is almost a proverb.
Education will not; the world is full of educated derelicts.
*Persistenc*e *and determination* alone are omnipotent."

—Calvin Coolidge

CHAPTER 13

The Missing Man

PAT EPPS AND I founded the Greenland Expedition Society (GES) in 1981. It's now nine years later, 1990, and we're in the middle of our sixth expedition of this endeavor. Currently, we have twelve guys plus Gina Pizzagalli on the ice cap – all hustling hard to bring a single P-38 Lightning fighter plane up through 260 feet of ice and snow to the surface of the glacier. The original ambition of recovering *all* of the planes has now been condensed to retrieving just one. Our excuse is, as we learn more about the scale of each engineering challenge, the total cost and elapsed time gets multiplied exponentially. Or something like that.

Because Pat and I both have businesses to run in Atlanta, we try to spell one another in the leadership

Captain William "Doug" Epps
9 Mar. 1929 – 2 Aug. 1990

15 of the 16 Dumbest Things I Have Ever Done in an Airplane

role on the ice cap. After having spent the last month and a half up there getting this year's operation set up and going, I have just returned to Atlanta to attend to some of those pressing business and domestic responsibilities. Pat is now in Greenland running things.

This morning, before heading out to my office, I'm here in the House of Tides (our family laundry room turned into a Ham radio shack). My house-phone rings and it's Pat's son, Patrick. He tells me that his uncle, Pat's brother, Doug Epps, just died unexpectedly of a heart attack here in Atlanta. Doug was a senior captain for Delta Air Lines and Chief Pilot for the GES. He was 60 years old.

Since I maintain daily contact with the operation on the cap through my HAM radio station, KC4FST, Patrick asks if I can get the message up to his dad.

I tell him, "As soon as we hang up."

Even as we're talking, my head is already buzzing with a dozen stories about Uncle Dougie. Even in GES's darker moments of mission failure (of which there were more than a few), he might sit back, whip out his harmonica, and blow a pretty mean "Turkey in the Straw." Then he might pull a small flask of Chivas Regal from his pocket, toss away the cork, and pass it around. The crazy thing about this was, I don't think any of us drank Scotch – and forget about drinking whiskey straight. But on those occasions with Uncle Dougie, we'd all take a ceremonial nip. I have no idea where the remaining three-quarters of those little bottles went.

When I hang up with Patrick, I make direct radio contact with Pat in Greenland. Before I sign off, I tell him that I want to arrange some kind of aerial celebration for Doug's funeral. He acknowledges my offer, but after hearing the tragic substance of this call, I'm not at all confident that he processes much else of what I have to say. Even with 3,000 miles of separation, I can feel the instant arc-flash in his heart followed by the hollow black hole left in his chest.

Right now, Pat needs space, not hand-holding. I sign off. My deep-hearted love for each of these guys compels me to get started on putting together something a little bit larger-than-life *for both of them*. And whatever it is, it needs to be performed at Uncle Dougie's scale of thinking and Pat's scale of brotherhood. The burial services are the day after tomorrow. This gives me today and tomorrow for preparation of whatever it's going to be. Not much time.

Uncle Dougie's *handle* on the ice cap is an appellation he bestowed upon himself – *"Captain Wide-Body."* Consequently, my first thought is to assemble a flight of four Boeing 747 jumbo jets to make a low-level, ceremonial flyby over the burial ceremonies. Think about it! The sky will be filled with thundering *wide bodies*. Their looming shadows will darken the already grieving services. The earth will tremble, and maybe some women will even swoon. But, by damn, *all* of our spirits will be moved!

Yes. A wide-body flyby is the answer!

My first telephone call is to a pilot-friend of mine who flies for Delta. He gives me the names of some of the airline's uppity-up executives. I'm confident that I can convince them to make the great "Captain Wide-body Flyby" happen. Obviously, it'll be significant PR for Delta. After conversations with two vice presidents who don't seem to share my enthusiasm, I ring up a higher-up guy, Mr. Harrison. Patiently, he hears me out, then replies, "No. Delta also grieves at losing one of our senior pilots, but think about the precedent it will set for all future pilots and staff dying from here on out. I'm sorry, Mr. Taylor, but I think you can understand our position."

Before I hang up, I thank him (sincerely) for his delicately handled lesson in simple corporate protocol. But within minutes, another notion pops up. Instead of a *wide-body flyby*, what about a *Missing Man Formation of only DC-3s?* Although this scotches the *wide-body* metaphor, we'll gain the Gooney Bird connection. In Uncle Dougie's eyes, this might even be better. Hell, it *is* better!

Since Pat is going to be busy with a ton of family duties, I take one minute to radio him back about the program, and that I'll handle it. He's agreeable.

The burial service is scheduled for 10:00 a.m. on August 4, 1990, and will be held at the big cemetery in Athens, Georgia. It's located about two miles east of the University of Georgia campus and just a mile and a half northwest of their airport.

Don Brooks buys a lot of his DC-3 parts from a friend of his, Bob McSwiggen. Bob owns Academy Airlines, an aviation cargo operation fifty miles south of Atlanta. They also operate three DC-3s they use for hauling heavy cargo. The Epps clan is the founding family of aviation in Georgia. So, of course, Bob knows all the Epps boys. I call to tell him that Doug died and that we need all three of his "Threes" to form a Missing Man formation in two days. There is not enough time to negotiate cost. I simply tell him that we'll be glad to pay full fare for fuel, pilots, and aircraft time if he can help us out on the day after tomorrow. He is totally agreeable to doing anything he can to help, but tells me that only two of his DC-3s are in Atlanta. But he agrees to have both of them at the Athens airport on August 4 at 0800. Almost parenthetically, he adds, "And by the way. The planes and associated expenses are *on the house*." This is a huge gift – especially because I have absolutely no idea how to pay for all this stuff. Thank you, again, Bob.

Pat arrives in Atlanta the next day, and I brief him on what's going on. I also mention that I'm still looking for one more DC-3 to make a three-plane formation. He doesn't know of any available 3s, but he calls his flight department and arranges for one of his Learjets to join us. Another one of his pilots who flies Epps's Mitsubishi MU-2 twin turboprop, hears about this Missing Man tribute. Naturally, he wants to be part of the performance as well. He calls Pat, and of course, Pat tells him *sure*, and to "just call Taylor." So here I am now with one rocket-fast private jet, one super-fast twin turboprop, and two lumbering cargo planes with big, noisy, propeller-driven radial engines – all in one big screwball batch.

But do you know what? Somehow this is turning out exactly the way it's all supposed to. Dougie's all inside my head – his blue eyes are twinkling, and he's just laughing his ass off. "Hell, Super, loosen up. The more, the merrier. Right?"

The night before the funeral, on my way home after work, I stop by a flower shop on Peachtree Street and buy a bushel basket of fresh red roses. This afternoon I had called a friend, Nathan Metzger. He owns a bright-yellow Piper Cub and agreed to do a treetop-level flyover at the gravesite tomorrow morning. His mission is to cast the rose petals over all the mourners at the ceremony. The flower-petal performance will be the traditional precursor to the now mixed-breed Missing Man formation. Nathan's flower strewing will be a metaphor for little angels sprinkling petals before Captain Widebody as he walks up to the Pearly Gates with that devil-may-care smile on his face. Or something like that.

Even though the symbolism gets pretty loosey-goosy here, all the mourners will be thinking that the Piper Cub and the rose petal thing is a quiet little emotional touch. But then will come the thundering drama of World War II cargo planes and noisy jet engines! All that flower-girl thing is just an emotional set-up.

It is the prelude to the *wave of great flying machines thundering over the horizon*. Even Genghis Khan would wet his pants at this *wham-bam, thank you, ma'am!*

15 of the 16 Dumbest Things I Have Ever Done in an Airplane

I can hear Uncle Dougie now: "Super, are you sure you know what in the hell you're doing? Do you need me to run get my gee-haw-whimmy-diddle? Or should I blow an 'Oh, Susanna' on my harp?"

Right now, I'm busy as hell and don't have time to listen to his distractions. I call the two DC-3 pilots, the two Epps's pilots, and Nathan on the phone and ask them to meet at the Athens airport for a pilot briefing at 0800 the next morning – Saturday. The flyby will be at 1000 hours sharp. The Learjer and Mitsubishi pilots don't answer their phones, so I leave voice messages that outline what's going on. Of course, I ask that they call me back and meet for the pilot's briefing.

Because street maps are easier to read than aviation charts, I spend the evening drawing up five flight plans on gas station type, fold-up, street maps. One map is for me. The layout includes the flight path, headings, altitudes, the course-reversal area, radio frequencies and a scramble plan in case anything goes awry.

Saturday, August 4, 1990

Neither one of the Epps pilots called me back last night, and they didn't answer my calls this morning. We've got to keep going. At 0700, with the basket of roses in the back seat, I fly my Bonanza the 50 miles over to Athens airport and get the petal-plucking operation going.

The Athens airport is named the Athens-Ben Epps Airport. Pat and his family all grew up in Athens, and, of course, Ben was Doug's and Pat's father.

Around the year 1907, Ben Sr. was the first person to fly an airplane in the State. This was an aircraft of his own design and construction – hence the airport name. Pat was three years old when his father was killed in a plane crash. All five of Pat's brothers and one of his three sisters became licensed pilots. I've always held that none of the Epps kids ever did learn to fly. They didn't have to. It was genetically encoded in their DNA. Like birds on the wing, they just do it.

Nathan arrives in his Piper Cub at the airport at 0800, and he and I go right to work plucking petals.

It's counter-intuitive until you try it, but pulling petals off a fresh rose blossom takes a lot more time than you'd think.

You picking up on all this, Dougie?

While plucking, I'm thinking. Since the 2 Epps's planes didn't show up, we've got to have a third plane, and mine's parked just outside on the apron. What choice is there but for me to join the fray. Besides, I've secretly wanted to do this since the very start of this thing. Also, I know damned good and well that Uncle Dougie wants this to happen this way. *I'll be the third man.* Perfect! We'll work out the details at our pilot's meeting later this morning.

At 0815, the two McSwiggen DC-3s land and park just outside the hangar where Nathan and I are already petal-plucking. Most agreeably, both new pilots come in, sit down, and help finish the deflowering operation. Once we get the product of our friendly tedium stuffed into two big black plastic garbage bags, we load them in the front seat in Nathan's Cub. He'll fly the plane from the back seat. Yes, there is a second set of controls back there.

With that task done, the four of us then go back in the hangar for our formal pilot briefing. I give each of the DC-3 pilots their hand annotated local road map. This Missing Man thing is not a complicated operation. It's simply new territory for all of us. The Piper Cub (flower girl) will get a twenty-minute head start. Nathan will fly directly to the gravesite and start circling and casting petals. It should take him only two minutes to get there. It will take another ten minutes (max) to cast the petals into his prop blast for dispersal. His performance will serve as the place marker for our Missing Man flight to target in on.

As we're loading the Cub, Nathan asks me, "Suppose there's a bunch of burying's going on? How am I going to know which is the correct one?" Of course, I don't know the answer, but he needs one right now, "Easy. Just pick the biggest one." I hope I'm right.

I then call for the pilot briefing and tell Nathan and the DC-3 pilots that I will fly my Bonanza in the third spot of the Missing Man. For squadron symmetry, I will fly between and behind the 2 big planes, but a shade higher to keep out of their prop blast and wing-tip vortices. Obviously, I don't mention it, but I secretly envision them as my chariot team. When we get over the grave site, I will then become the one who peels out of the back of the formation. This symbolizes the honored pilot leaving his buddies and, in the old aviator's tradition, "heads west."

At 0930, Nathan cranks up his Cub and flies over to the cemetery. We're exactly on schedule.

At 0940, as a flight of two, the DC-3s take off. I follow immediately behind them. To get comfortable with our formation flying, we'll fly 12 miles out, make a 180-degree turn, then fly back to the burial ceremony. The outbound leg will be flown at 1000 feet. After we make the 180 at this altitude, we'll then descend down to 500 feet. The need for the low altitude pass is to enhance the maximum engine-rumble effect.

I haven't mentioned it to anyone yet, but as I leave the formation and "fly west," as a final salute to Dougie, I may also do a low-level Victory Roll. Five hundred feet is a little low to roll a six-seat, non-aerobatic business aircraft. But if you do it right, there should be no problem. I've done plenty of rolls in this plane, but none of them so low that I could see people down there standing around looking up at me.

We're off and as I'm beginning to form up with the DC-3s, the Learjet, from somewhere I can't see, calls me on the UNICOM radio frequency and announces that he's got us in sight and that the Epps MU-2 is on his wing-tip! Oh, man! They missed the briefing and don't have charts! But no matter how jack-legged this thing sounds, I know damn-good-and-well that we are somehow going to fold them into the show. That's a given.

Because it doesn't seem like a good idea to execute the coordinated 180-degree turn as a *five-plane* formation, I tell both Epps pilots to just slow down and join the party right *after* the DC-3s and I make our inbound turn to the cemetery. I then tell the DC-3 pilots to extend our turnaround location for one more minute. That's about two miles. But it will also delay us by three minutes for the flyover schedule. I hate being late, but that's just the way it's gotta be.

The DC-3s and I complete our 180 and are now inbound to the cemetery. I instruct the Lear to suck up to the right wing of the right DC-3 and to hold that wing-tip as tight as he can at his ten-o'clock position. I then give the MU-2 the left wing-tip of the other DC-3. Then I call the Learjet pilot *only* and tell him to be ready *at my call* to punch in full power for a max angle of climb straight up and into the wild blue yonder above. I will give him a short-count to *"Break."* I tell him to keep going up until he disappears out of sight. Then he's on his own. He symbolizes the wake-up call to everybody up there in heaven to just *hold on, our man* is on his way.

He acknowledges these instructions with two clicks of his mic. That's pretty classy, but I wished he'd have answered in plain English. Keeping track of everybody melding together has caused me to lag behind the formation. With 20 seconds of full throttle, I catch up to my spot in the middle of the pack. We have good symmetry. The air is butter-smooth.

15 of the 16 Dumbest Things I Have Ever Done in an Airplane

My flock is finally lined up four-abreast for the final approach over the gravesite. I feel like a sheepdog who's done his job. I don't have to bark or nip at anybody.

At the pilot briefing, I made up a rule that except in an emergency, nobody is to talk on the radio, except me. Everyone is respecting that rule, and now the no-conversation between any of the five pilots feels awkward. The gag rule was probably not a necessary restriction. At two miles (one minute) north of the cemetery, we're a tight formation at 500 feet above the ground. This is less than the height of the Washington Monument.

The sky is an unspoiled blue, and there's no wind. The formation stays militarily tight and quiet. I hear nothing but the steady drone of my trusty Bonanza motor.

At one mile north of the ceremony, we're still damn near perfect. The DC-3s are setting a textbook pace at a steady 140 knots. I notice that the Lear has its flaps extended ten or maybe fifteen degrees, but at least its landing gear is up. All of us, except for Nathan below us, (and me a little above), are holding the 500-foot altitude.

All the mourners at the ceremony should be starting to hear our thunder coming up on them. As we get closer to the cemetery, we can now see the assemblage of all the decked-out people looking up at us. Although my eyes are constantly checking the distances between the four planes in front of me, I do take a one-microsecond flicker-glance at the crowd. It's huge. I think I saw some petals still fluttering about, but I simply don't have time to look at anything except the immediate brace of airplanes spread out in front of me.

Just as our five-man formation approaches the open grave, I radio, "Learjet only. Ready. Five. Four. Three. Two. One. Break!"

The Learjet firewalls the throttles, retracts his flaps, lowers its tail and punches up and out at a maximum rate of climb. He's trailing a straight-line wisp of grey exhaust. In just seconds, he's only a dot, heaven-bound. The roar of his jet exhaust is pointed directly back at the funeral gathering. The guests may, or may not be impressed. But I am in total awe!

Look out, angels! Here comes Uncle Dougie's flagman!

Nathan was supposed to have vacated the area several minutes ago, but he's still circling the congregation at just above treetop level. Call it a hundred feet. Because most of the petals kept blowing back in his face and filling up the back of the airplane, he was flying with the control stick between his knees and had to keep making repeated turns over the crowd to finish the job.

In only a matter of a few seconds, the gravesite comes up under our nose. If I'm going to do this Victory Roll thing, it's gotta be right now – or forget it. My eyes follow the yellow Cub as I ease the Bonanza over to the right side of the right DC-3, and into the slot vacated by the Learjet. Then I push the nose of the plane down to accelerate. Simultaneously, I go to climb power to pick up the extra airspeed necessary for a roll. For this maneuver to work at low altitude, it must be executed fast and confidently – like you know what you're doing. There is no room for timidity. You simply clear your mind of all clutter (like all this stuff I'm describing here) and just do it.

I continue to push the nose down until the airspeed indicator needle touches the yellow caution mark on the dial. At the exact instant of that quick kiss, I pull back on the control wheel to bring the nose up about 30 degrees above the horizon. Simultaneously, I force the control wheel over to the right, all the way to its stop. Then hold it there. Very quickly, I'm exactly inverted. To buy back a few more feet of altitude, I give the nose a little forward pressure. This makes me a shade lighter in the seat, but I'm still positive G's. Then, as I continue the rollover to right-side-up, I end up level with the right DC-3 off my left wing-tip and a little behind me. I'm also heading nearly thirty degrees farther off course to the right. Apparently, I kept favoring away from the 3s a little too much. The good news is that I didn't run into either one of the two big airplanes or the MU-2 or the Piper Cub, or *Mother Earth or any of her mourners* below.

It all clicked. But before I let myself spool-down too much, I call the other five pilots to thank them for their participation in this event. In turn, they each radio back with thanks for including them. They then head home. This impersonal dispersal of our little squadron feels too soon and awkward. We are forever a brotherhood of pilots hastily thrown together. *And we nailed our mission.* Simply flying home our separate ways seems unfulfilling, or something awkward. I want to tell each of the other pilots an Uncle Dougie story. Something feels lonely right now. I can't really explain it.

It has been nine years since Pat showed me how to roll a plane. But for sure, he will smile at the good news thing about not running into anything today.

Of course, later today, I'll tell him that the thirty-degree exit maneuver was just part of the Missing Man lore. He'll smile, but he'll know. And that's all just the way it's supposed to be.

It only takes twenty minutes to fly back to PDK. That's still not enough time to spool down. Nancy and the kids won't be back for an hour or so. After I park the Bonanza in its hangar, I clean off bugs, tidy the interior, and sweep the concrete floor that doesn't really need sweeping.

While just putzing around, I'm thinking that Uncle Dougie is still absolutely busting his britches. Maybe he just discovered that on the back of his tombstone, his daughter, Susan, had engraved, "Off on Another Adventure." He might also have found the bottle of Chivas that his family tucked in his casket. Surer'n the dickens, he will smile at that loving humor. Then he'll wonder, *What the hell do you do with the cork up here? Just toss it off the cloud?*

This morning's acknowledgment of the departure of a man well-loved is a small gesture by family and friends to a life well-lived. There is absolutely no way for me to adequately express how proud I am to be a part of it.

CHAPTER 14

DC-3, P I C

MAY 4, 1992
Although the title of this book pitches the possible merits of *arguable judgements in the pursuit of aviation*, this chapter may challenge the underlying foundation of that premise. On the other hand, this chapter storyline feels so much like mischief that it still fits right in. See if you agree.

Let's start with the stage-set of this episode – a World War II Douglas C-47, cargo plane.[18]

The C-47 line of aircraft started life in 1935 as a DC-3. DC stands for "Douglas Commercial." Their loading capacity, speed and reliability set them apart from the rest of the commercial field. They could fly the 800 miles from New York to Chicago in four hours flat whilst serving a tasty lunch and a cool nap. When the US entered the War in 1941, they immediately became the backbone of our military operation. Altogether, 11,000 of these workhorses were produced.

---

[18] Just to keep our designations straight, C-47 was the military designation for what civilians call a DC-3. Don Brooks, who lent the use of his plane to the Greenland Expedition Society, calls his plane a DC-3. Now, so do the rest of us.

The actual plane used in this chapter has a special history. On June 6, 1944, it carried twenty-eight young US Army paratroopers over the English Channel to jump into France preceding the Normandy Invasion on D-Day.[19] The troopers went on to fight the Battle of the Bulge.

At the time of this epic event, I was a nine-year-old paper boy delivering *The Washington Post* in the Maryland suburbs of Washington, DC. Before I rolled the papers into a log-shapes to toss up to my customer's doorsteps, I would religiously read the War headlines. That's how news was handled before TV took over. And even now, a few of us old goats with a few memory cells still popping, remember D-Day, VE Day, Hiroshima and VJ Day. All of this is to say that Don Brook's DC-3 is not just another airplane.

Today we're headed north to Greenland on our seventh expedition to the ice cap. This is the third tour that Don Brooks has offered the GES the use of this highly venerated, ski-equipped DC-3. Expeditions One through Four were flown in either chartered ski planes or regular corporate-type aircraft – types that we are all certified to fly. Obviously, piloting a DC-3 requires experience not normally practiced in everyday aircraft. Nonetheless, every pilot, ranging from a moon-walking astronaut to the officer flying left seat in Air Force One, would covet the opportunity to fly a DC-3. She is the venerated Queen Mother of Aviation.

---

[19] As a personal aside, right out of high school, I joined the Army as an infantry grunt and became a Korean War vet. My only military schools of higher learning were Advanced Infantry and Jump School with the 82nd Airborne Division at Fort Bragg, NC. I only made 10 jumps, but, like chronic hives, variant forms of that deep-rooted paratrooper virus keep coming back.

Greenland Expedition Society DC-3
(Skis are retracted)

Today we're headed up to the ice cap with several tons of expedition equipment and eight hardy souls on board. The fuselage is so packed that it has become a formidable obstacle course just to get from the cargo door up to the cockpit. We are "over-gross" by several tons

Our goal this year is to melt enough holes in a row in the ice cap to create a slot measuring five by twenty feet that goes down 260 feet to the Lockheed P-38 Lightning we located in 1990. This fighter plane, along with her seven sister ships, has been hibernating there for the last half century. Once the melting of the

15 of the 16 Dumbest Things I Have Ever Done in an Airplane

ice shaft is completed, all of the guns and aircraft components will be hoisted up and loaded into the DC-3, and then shipped or flown back to the States for reassembly.

Currently, we are refueling at Schefferville Airport, Quebec Provence, Canada. This almost-abandoned, iron-mining town lies way up there somewhere, but not quite yet to the Arctic Circle. No roads run north from here. To get us this far, Pat was PIC and I flew copilot. Right now, my immediate mission in life is to get the crew fed. Yes, making lunch-runs for the crew is all part of the second-class citizenship in the copilot job description.

As everyone is finishing-off the hamburgers I just picked up in town thirty minutes ago, Pat hollers at me, "Okay. Lez go! Super, you drive!" I've been busy resecuring some of the equipment in the back of the plane and had just taken my first bite out of my not-very-good-to-begin-with and already-cold-burger. In one movement, I swallow what's in my mouth, crush the rest back into its wax-paper wrapper, squash it all in my jacket pocket, and muscle my way forward to the cockpit.

Just to be sure, I confirm with Pat, "You *do* mean left seat, don't you?"

"Yeah, let's get going." Obviously, he's in one of his no-nonsense, *go modes.*

I ask, "What about a preflight?"

"I've already done it. Lez go."

I'm thinking, *If Pat says he has done a preflight, then he's done a preflight.* The next question is, *is it a certified FAA preflight, or is it a Klondike "lez go" preflight?*

The engines are still ticking from the cooling-down process they started an hour ago. As I left the airport to scare up food for everybody, I did see him checking the oil in number two engine. Pat knows airplanes. That's good enough for me.

After I strap into the left seat and put on a headset, Pat says, "I'll crank the engines."

I tell him, "Oh no, no, no, man. I know the drill."

He acknowledges with an almost imperceptible little nod and points his forefinger at me. I then put my left hand out the window and point to our lineman standing under the nose of the plane with a giant fire extinguisher at his side. He nods an acknowledgement and gives me a thumbs-up. I thumbs-up back. Then Pat reads the Before-Start Checklist to get the plane all trimmed up and ready to start.

The actual starting process then begins. As is the tradition, I crank the starboard engine first by setting the throttle controls and pushing the overhead right starter switch to the up position. My right hand stays on the throttle. The giant three-bladed prop growls and starts rotating slowly. As each propeller blade passes the copilot's window, through the headset, I hear Epps counting, "One, two, three, …" At twelve, he again points to me. All cylinders should now have a little swallow of fuel. With my left hand, I carefully lift into place, *not flip*,[20] the magneto switch and then quickly reach over to blip the primer toggle-switch. With a serious rumble, the engine fires up willingly.

Then the left engine turns through its twelve blades, and it, too, eagerly thunders to life. This second engine start is on my side of the plane where I can look back and see the volumes of billowing white smoke blowing astern. The great smoke event adds visual drama that makes you take a breath. I carefully ease both throttles back to an exact 800-rpm idle. The matched pair of engines now loaf over smooth and clean. They also feel ready to exercise their mighty potential.

---

[20] You don't *flip* switches in old airplanes. You reposition them. Old plastic is brittle.

Both oil-pressure gauges read normal – exact center of the green. The engine-temp gauges are also still in the green. Fuel pressure is normal. We now have 2400 horsepower ready and willing to pull us north.

Taxiing the Douglas DC-3 is more art than science. The other pilots (each of whom I have silently judged harshly) have been jabbing the brakes to steer the plane. I am determined to make smoother, easier use of the brakes. I'm going to be the new Captain Smooth. Everybody back there in the hold somewhere will notice this quality right off. Then, the first time I cautiously ease in on the top of the rudder-pedals (the brakes), the plane jumps and jerks exactly as it did for everybody else.

Nobody says a word of criticism. Hell. They don't even notice! Apparently, this is simply an idiosyncrasy of this plane.

After running up the RPMs on each engine to check the magnetos, Pat radios the tower and gets us a clearance for take-off. I taxi this wonderfully complex yet obedient machine out to the end of the runway and swing around to line up exactly on its centerline. In my head, I recite, "Dead foot, dead engine."[21] Holding the brakes firmly, I push both throttles forward enough to bring the power up to twenty-eight inches of mercury in the intake manifold pressure gauge. This gauge measures how hard each engine is working, and also shows if they are humming in harmony with one another. Both engines feel equally *willing and eager*. Another quick scan of the twenty or so gauges in the panel – everything looks good. I release the brakes by sliding my feet down to the big part of the rudder pedals. As we start rolling,

---

[21] It has happened before. When one engine loses power, pilots have made the mistake of inadvertently feathering, or shutting down, the running engine. Hence, this little mental drill. If an engine in flight shuts down, the pilot intuitively corrects the directional change in heading with hard rudder pressure. The other foot becomes your dead foot. The dead-foot engine is the one to feather and shut down.

I ease the throttles on up to forty-eight inches on the manifold gauge – *full power*. Keep in mind that this airplane is nearly as long as an eighteen-wheeler, and with the load we have on board, weighs nearly as much.

At 25 knots, and still not airborne, I give a little forward pressure on the control wheel to lift the tail. It elevates slowly but obediently. In just a few more seconds, the fuselage is level with the runway – and we're now accelerating on those big, fat, main-gear tires. The tail is flying. The wings – not yet. Steering is performed only with the rudder pedals. I hold her here in this balanced position – nice and level. We keep accelerating on the centerline of the runway. Both engines are breathing full-throat and sound healthy. Oh, man, this is good. My every sensitivity is now in my fingertips. They're just waiting to feel her want to fly. Come on, baby!

Just as the airspeed indicator needle touches 80 knots, I feel a hint of lightness. She just took a baby-breath. With the gentlest more back-pressure on the control wheel, I encourage her to do it again. She catches the clue and just like it was her idea all along, gently severs her allegiance to Mother Earth and offers it to me. Pat's left hand is still on top of my right one, which is on the two throttle levers between us. I take a quick glance over to his right hand to be sure he's not cheating and shadowing me on the controls. He's not. He's scanning the engine gauges just like a good *copilot* should. Everything is exactly the way it's supposed to be.

I call, "Gear up," and won't begin to try to explain the visceral power of saying those two words.

He replies, "Gear up," and goes right into the same retraction routine I've done for him so many times.

The weather is clear, smooth, and cool – just about perfect. Pat locks the landing gear in the *up position*, sets the engine RPMs, fuel mixture, and manifold pressure for cruise-climb, then adjusts the cowl flaps to keep the cylinder temperatures exactly right. We keep our steady climb. He performs my old job just as effortlessly as I always tried to make it look. As he reads the After Takeoff Checklist to me, I notice that he checks my every response like he doesn't trust my answers. Actually, this is exactly what all good copilots do.

After we get up to cruise altitude –7,000 feet, this whole takeoff procedure starts to sink in. Because I'm not going to spill all my emotions out right here, I will only remind you that a very important aspect of flying is technical. *But the big part is spiritual.* And if you want to know what that means, read *Night Flight* by Antoine de Saint-Exupery. He'll take you right up there on a black, starry night in Argentina and bring tears of otherworldly wonder to your eyes.

However, if you're young and still need immediate gratification, read *High Flight* by John Gillespie Magee. In fact, read it a couple of times. One time is not enough.

Even after we're set up at cruise configuration, Epps still watches everything (including me) with the unblinking determination of a fearless mother hawk. He's still not talking much. The scattered clouds and arctic blue sky up ahead stay postcard perfect. The terrain below is desolate and appears totally untampered with. As far as we can see, there is an endless series of frozen lakes covered with what looks like a huge white comforter of snow. We've not yet reached *the tree line,* so endless forests of evergreens still run over the horizon in all directions. Arctic Canada is huge, elegant, and from this altitude, completely unblemished by human breath, love, hate, greed or fingerprint.

After an hour, Neil Estes moves up into the cockpit and takes Pat's place in the right seat. This is good. Neil and I have been friends for decades and share a bunch of crazy stories. Today we're not reminiscing. Since he's a pilot and rated in the DC-3, our flying this plane together today will add another page to our curious journal of ventures – stuff ranging from my designing – and him building – several huge arts festivals in Atlanta, to our racing motorcycles against one another, handlebar to handlebar.

After passing Kuujjuaq, Quebec, the Hudson Straight comes up on the horizon ahead. This overwater flight takes nearly an hour. There isn't much water showing. It's 90 percent pack-ice. Way up ahead, the harsh, snow-covered black rocks of Baffin Island are a welcome sight. But in terms of hospitality, it offers damn near nothing. Also, because we are now north of the tree line, there aren't any more of those comfortable remembrances either.

At fifty miles out from our destination, Iqaluit (formerly Frobisher Bay), I radio ahead with our position report. Pat moves back into the copilot seat and reads the In-Range Check List. Once we have this formal protocol out of the way, he feels the need to get back to running things. "All you gotta do is hold ninety-five knots till you get over the threshold, then level out and ease back on the throttles, and you're there. Oh yeah, and don't stop flying until you stop rolling."

There is no question that this last remark about "stop rolling" relates to the ground loop I performed in his Cessna only *four years ago*[22]. Forgive and forget? Yeah, right!

He then adds, "If it starts to get away from you, I'll take it."

To this I have to respond, "Don't even think about it, Klondike. This is going to be a *paint job*. All you need to do is get your scorecard out and sharpen your pencil."

At fifteen miles from the airport, I dial in the localizer/glide-slope navigation frequency. This instrument is required to make an instrument approach in bad visibility. Even though we're making a visual approach today, and don't need their assist,

---

[22] A ground loop is an unintentional and uncontrolled spinning of a taildragger at the moment of landing.

I want to play the full game and monitor all of the dials – just because I can. Plus, it should help keep the boundaries of the approach nice and tight. Approach Control calls the prevailing wind as straight down the runway at 15 knots, gusting to 22. It's right on our nose and about the upper reaches of the comfort zone. If it's accurate, there will be no crosswind to contend with. This is a gift. The headwind will slow down our *ground* speed, which works a little to our advantage. Because our ground speed will be nearly 20 mph slower, it will take just a tad more power to stay on the glide slope,

At three miles out, we're *on the glide slope* and in perfect alignment with the runway. The airspeed needle is pegged at 95 knots. We start to sink a bit below the glide slope needle, but I catch it easily by adding just a shade of additional throttle. As soon as the sink stops, I throttle back an equal shade – nice and easy-like. The approach stays centered. Ever so gradually, however, we've now inched a needle's width above the glide path. Normally I'd just leave it there, but with Mama Hawk sitting right here next to me, watching everything with those beady eyes, this must be perfect. I ease back the littlest bit on the throttles and hold the nose up just a tad. The airspeed slowly bleeds down to 80 knots. I then hold the plane off from descending any farther with just the smallest increase of back pressure. I just want to hold her here nice and steady for a few moments. Stall speed for this plane is 58 knots. But, since we're considerably over gross allowable weight, I'm adding an additional 10-knot safety-margin. Then, before I'm actually ready for it, *chirp!* Damn it! I didn't expect touchdown just yet. Reflexively, I release a little back pressure on the controls to *plant* the main gear. The big tires stay pegged on the runway; no bounce, no float! We're now just rolling along smartly with the tail as straight back as a carpenter's level.

Pat comes over my headset again, almost like he's talking to himself or sharing a secret with me. "Ease the throttles all the way back." His soft dialogue sounds like he's trying to be my subconscious or something. Besides, I was already pulling them back.

But it ain't over yet. No matter how caustic Epps's earlier admonishment of, "Don't stop flying until you stop rolling," might have seemed, in landing a taildragger, it's fundamental gospel truth.

With a little more forward control pressure, I still have enough airspeed to hold the tail up. Steering straight down the runway with rudder up in the air is easy. That is until the elevator of the airplane loses lift and the tail eases itself down on its own. The tailwheel now starts participating in the steering program. The plane's nose starts hunting to the left; I catch it with a jab of right rudder. The whole airplane then starts pointing to the right. I catch it – actually, a little better than before. Pat is still low-tone conversational. "Hit your rudder at the first sign of movement – stay ahead of it." In microseconds, everything is realigned – oh, man, what a feeling this is. The big airplane now stays on all three wheels aligned to the runway in complete homage to her tenderfoot aircraft commander.

Don Brooks and Neil have been standing directly behind Pat and me in the cockpit throughout this whole landing procedure. They start clapping and patting the PIC on the shoulders. The applause sounds so good that I start clapping too. Pat pays zero attention to the spontaneous celebration and starts tidying up the cockpit like he's bored to death and finally found something worthy of his lofty attention.

Obviously, this flight makes a great entry in my Pilot Logbook Number 6. But, to me it's so much more than that. It's one of the more notable benchmarks in this one man's life.

After we shut-down under the control tower, and since I didn't screw up, I now need to share all this excitement with the guys riding in the back of the plane. Half of them are pilots. After the plane's parked, I finally work my way aft to where everybody is busy rummaging through piles of cargo, looking for their personal gear. Maybe all that praise and awe for today's conspicuous flying achievement will simply have to wait till happy hour. Actually, this sounds a little bit better anyway. I'll wait. Hell, to prime the pump, I'll even buy the first round!

After all the guys and equipment are unloaded, Pat and Neil taxi the plane over to the overnight parking area a couple of hundred yards from the terminal building. I check in at the Flight Service desk to do the paper work, order gas and close our flight plan. By the time I'm finished, everybody else has wandered off somewhere. Maybe they found a bar or something. The hotel is less than a mile from the terminal, and since I really would like some *alone time*, I pick up my personal gear and walk alone over to the Navigator Inn to make arrangements for our accommodations. On the way, I take the uneaten hamburger out of my jacket pocket and feed it to an aggressive, yelping Huskey that's tied to a gate post. Somehow feeding the dog feels like a metaphor for something, but I can't figure it out.

At the Inn, I book four rooms and go stretch out in Pat's and mine. Some twenty minutes later, *in two taxi cabs*, the rest of the crew finally roll in. Everybody dumps their respective gear in their assigned room and, ten minutes later, we all head next door to our favorite Canadian hangout. The Canadian Legionnaires remember us and welcome us aboard. Everything still looks and smells about the same. A third of the fifty patrons here appear to be of indigenous ancestry. Several come to our table selling green soapstone carvings of polar bears and seals. Their prices range from forty to seventy-five Canadian dollars. Some of the sculpture work is expressive and of excellent quality.

DC-3, P I C

As I had planned, I buy the table the first round of beers, (except for Pat, who prefers a half glass of any kind of cheap white wine). Now I wait patiently for somebody to bring the conversation around to the conspicuously incredible DC-3 landing event they all just enjoyed just a little bit ago. For some reason, it doesn't happen. I can't believe it. Don Brooks buys the second round, and the conversation simply continues to center on trivial stuff like the expedition, or how cold it was in the back of the plane, or whatever. A few guys have a third round and then we all head back over to the Navigator dining room for a big supper. It's not a three-minute walk, but in that brief period of time, I make a resolution, to wit:

"The incredible story of the *World's Greatest Aircraft Landing in the Recorded History of Aviation* is hereby left to stew (and possibly ferment) in the beer-softened cerebral cortex of the way-too-swollen head now residing on the feature pilot's shoulders. And right now, that's probably the right place for it to simmer-out. But, inasmuch as that pilot is now recording this event in this journal tonight, it's probably wisest to just let it slide into anonymous, half-life decay. Perhaps it may 'stay at rest until disturbed by an outside force'[23] sometime in the future – maybe."

But it could turn out to be like that old story of the guy walking along a beach after a great storm. The beech is littered with many thousands of washed-up star fish. Every step or so, he leans over and throws one back into the ocean. Another guy comes along and says, "Why are you bothering to throw those starfish back? There are so many of them that it won't make any difference." The first fellow picks up another starfish and throws it into the sea, and says, "It will to this one."

That last starfish was me!
So endeth of lesson.

---
[23] Newton's first law of motion

CHAPTER 15

You Haven't Failed Until You Quit

NOTE: THE FOLLOWING event is significantly out of sequence with the other tribunals shared in this book. It took place at the wrap-up of our second, *failed* GES Expedition to the Greenland ice cap in 1981. At that time, its message was perfect-timing for our searching for lost airplanes. For this book about a variety of aviation activities, however, its *anchor position* seems to me to be more appropriate. In any event, here goes...

Sondrestrom International Airport, Greenland
October 22, 1981, 2300 hours local.

Even though we're reloading our never-even-opened expedition equipment back in the airplane in a dark corner of the airport on a royally gloomy night, we're trying to keep our spirits at least civil. The string of runway lights only a couple of hundred yards away contribute little useful luminance to this *tail-between-our-legs* departure. This is our *second* failed expedition to find the Lost

Squadron somewhere out there on the Greenland Ice Cap. Right now, Pat Epps is filing our flight plan, and I'm getting the plane loaded and ready to head back to Atlanta. Norman Vaughan, our venerated Arctic explorer, and Bruce Bevin, our geophysicist, are helping me with the heavy lifting chores. Russell Rajani, head of Pursuits Unlimited, our corporate partner, is handling his own gear.

The plane we're flying was lent to us by Pat's good friend, Richard Beacham. It's a Cessna Citation – *his private jet, no less!* I had to get checked out in it the week before we left... Oh, the sacrifices we sometimes have to make!

But more importantly, how do you ever say *thank you* enough for Beacham's magnitude of generosity? Well, I'll tell you. You can't. I'll also tell you that if your mission fails, as ours just did, it's even more difficult.

Today was an absolute unabashed bummer. But, in a nutshell, it went something like this: We took off early this morning from this very same airport in a chartered, ski-equipped de Havilland Twin Otter. We hired it to take us to the presumed location of the Lost Squadron crash site on the other side of Greenland – some 350 miles east of here.

When the Twotter got to the general area of the buried planes, the ice cap's surface was being eviscerated by winds so high that even *if* a ski-landing were survivable, the possibility of *shooting the sun* to obtain geographic coordinates for subsequent pickup would not be possible. The surface of the cap was being completely anointed to some unknown depth by swirling globs of creamy topping. It was impossible to determine the depth of either the blowing stuff or the new accumulation. We had no reasonable choice but to return here to Sondrestrom.[24]

---

[24] As an interesting note, in the subsequent five expeditions the Greenland Expedition Society will make to Greenland, this level of

Once back here, a thorough review at Greenland's central weather station offered no reasonable glimmer of hope for us to linger here waiting for incremental improvements on the other side of the island.

It's a painful decision, but we're now cowering our way back to the colorful autumn climes of Atlanta, Georgia – one hell of a lot wiser about who ultimately runs the show up here, and another $35,000 poorer.

Nonetheless, this day's schooling in Classic Arctic Magic is not yet over. We don't know it yet, but a heavenly finale is now being programmed for a grand showing a little later tonight.

But right now, as we are loading what feels like a ton of heavy technical equipment back aboard the plane, I'm thinking about how to explain this second failure to everybody back home. There's Nancy and the kids, friends, business partners and curious clients. They're all rooting for us. The determined confidence at our departure only four days ago will surely be remembered upon our not-so-grandiose return tomorrow.

As for loading the plane, Norman Vaughan, our celebrity partner, is hefting more than his share of the load. Because of his arctic experience and, quite frankly, his confidence and leadership, we asked him to join us. He never tries to run the show, but everyone in his company is always fully aware of his exceptional experience and senior presence.

Norman's history here in Greenland goes back to 1942. He was dropped off on the eastern coastline of the island by a US Coast Guard cutter and drove a team of dogs inland to the freshly abandoned squadron. His mission was to retrieve a secret Norden bombsight that had been inadvertently left behind in one of the two bombers that crashed landed there. (The crew of the other bomber exploded their bombsight before they were rescued.)

---

caution will seldom be respected. This correct call was simply fortuitously insightful.

15 of the 16 Dumbest Things I Have Ever Done in an Airplane

The balance of his polar resumé includes accompanying Admiral Byrd to Antarctica on his great expedition in 1929 to fly to the South Pole. Norman's incredible background, coupled with extraordinary personal grace, makes his presence on this current expedition iconic. Of course, he's handsome, athletic, intelligent, engaging, courteous, and Harvard-trained. He's of a stocky build, with a full head of hair. Even shaven, he carries the mantle of an arctic explorer.

On every hectic day of preparing for this trip, and after my personal oomph-needle has already started its normal dip, his energy level stays full-tilt. He's seventy-eight years old, but looks no more than sixty. He works like he's even younger than that.

On the other hand, he also possesses a personal quality that can, under certain circumstances, test a lesser man's patience. To wit: sometimes, he will softly whistle to himself when performing a menial task. You know – like in the middle of a cold, dark Arctic night, while loading a poorly lit airplane fully shrouded in the solemn drapes of failure, *he'll whistle to himself.*

So here we are – only a few hours after our aborted attempt to land the Twotter at the site, and everybody's mood is subdued and almost mechanical. That is, everybody's except Norman's. The rest of us are trying not to look like poor losers. But he's whistling like everything is just hunky-dory! I hate to say it, but his dispassion for the gravity of the moment feels a little insensitive to me. He and I need to have a *mano a mano.*

I finish stuffing my sleeping bag way in the back of the dark cabin of the plane and then go over to him standing at the passenger door.

I start right in. "Goddamn it, Norman, don't you realize that we're *wimping it* back to Atlanta. We've just failed – *again*! And don't you understand that we have simply pissed away another boatload of money and don't have a damn thing to show for it? So how in the name of hell can anybody be out here in the freezing-ass cold, whistling like everything's just peachy?"

Norman stands solidly, about nose to nose with me. He lets my venting go uninterrupted. When I'm finished, he continues his pause for another long moment before he says anything. At least it's long enough that I have enough time to hear a little replay of what I just said.

Then, in an even voice, he answers, "Well, Richard, I hear what you're saying. And I understand what you're feeling." His large eyes are so locked onto mine that there's no way for me to look away.

He goes on almost cautiously, "I see the effort we just made differently from what you see. I see that we have come a long way to get to Greenland. Then, when we got here, we went straight into the teeth of the gale. And we went as far as man could go. We followed every avenue of opportunity and turned every stone that could be turned. We didn't fail, and we have absolutely nothing to be ashamed of. And, more importantly, *we haven't failed until we quit.* Yes, we just had a setback. But that's a long way from failure. Now, Richard. Let me get this straight. You're not suggesting to me that we just quit, are you?"

How can I be such easy pickings? Even before the midpoint of this epic little speech, I see the whole game. It's just like your classic chess gambit – as soon as your opponent touches his piece to respond to your last move, you see your last mistake like a rifle report. In just that half-a-heartbeat, it's all so obvious.

For me, at least, Norman just disarmed one of the biggest of any of our mortal enemies; that is, *the fear of failure* and the *shame of humiliation* that goes with it. In thirty seconds here in this dark cold night, Norman reshaped our returning home, empty-handed (for a second time), into a laudable victory.

Since our discussion is not yet over, I still have to answer his question about quitting. "Of course not, Norman. No, we're not quitting. I guess I just got caught up in the moment."

I hate it, but I'm still only human. And since I still must hang on to my last thread of personal pride, I add, "Well. How 'bout just not whistling then? Okay?"

His facial expression has been focused and serious. It softens, but only slightly. He doesn't capitulate. You'd have to be quick to even catch any change all. But I can see right now that I'm not going to get off this hook unscathed.

He doesn't answer me.

The entire brace of imaginary cameras now turns back on me.

Since my pitiful little bag of mental gymnastics is empty, I reach out to shake hands. What a doopy thing to do. I hope, without saying it, that this is my way of saying *I'm sorry*. But I'm not begging. In return, Norman's handshake is strong. It says, without his verbalizing it, *we're okay*. Neither one of us verbalizes a compromise to end this little tête-à-tête. We don't do that. We don't need to.

Our deep and sincere friendship just got another layer of long-term bonding-agent.

So, here I am left just standing by the door, still shivering-ass cold, thinking I'm about the luckiest guy in the whole damned world.

Now figure that one out.

In another ten minutes, the Citation is loaded. Pat's pilot. I'm in the right seat. Our flight plan calls for departing Sondrestrom, Greenland, and flying direct to Goose Bay, Labrador. It's a thousand-mile flight almost entirely over water along the north–south axis of the Davis Strait. This is the iceberg-laced body of water that separates Greenland from Canada. For most of the flight, we will be several hundred miles from either coastline.

Sonde Control Tower clears us for takeoff shortly before midnight. The weather is 1,200-foot overcast, 19° F, and surface winds at 25 knots from the west.

Half an hour later, we're at thirty-two thousand feet and midway between Greenland and Canada. There's no moon tonight.

The night sky is clear, with an incredible canopy of stars spreading all the way down to a hard-edged, black horizon. There are no human-generated lights anywhere.

Norman and Bruce Bevin sit in the two seats behind Pat and me. Russell Rajani is in the passenger seat behind them.

Shortly after take-off, there seems to be a problem with the heating system in the plane. It's gotten cold in here. It must be serious because Epps turns the plane over to me as he pulls out the Pilot's Operating Manual. He finds a work-around in the heating system and gets it to blast very *hot* and *very loud* air into the cabin. It's not thermostatically controlled. It's either full-on or full-off. This is annoying, but sure beats the hell out of freezing to death. The outside air temp at this altitude is -65° F. Everyone still has their sweaters, boots, coats, hats and scarves on.

Other than the two jet engines back there just blowing their little hearts out, there's nothing else going on.

Epps takes the plane back so he can go back to watching the autopilot do the flying. I go back to fiddling with the radios to see if I can get any response from anybody. No luck.

Plotting this course home is easy. Civil aviation doesn't have a Global Positioning System (GPS) yet, so just like Christopher Columbus five hundred years ago, we're just steering by following a rather unsteady magnetic compass that seeks every opportunity to point to anything except its primary homing target, the Magnetic North Pole. The "Mag Pole's" location, incidentally, is several hundred miles behind us and getting farther away at the rate of about 350 miles per hour.

Try though I might, I cannot make radio contact with anyone. There is not even a distant warble of man-made electronic generation. Except for our intermittent, roaring heat-blasts, everything is quiet and peaceful.

15 OF THE 16 DUMBEST THINGS I HAVE EVER DONE IN AN AIRPLANE

A few little specks of iceberg glitter below us competes with the star canopy above. For the nocturnal glamour award, the stars win easily.

Another hour passes with intermittent, two-minute blasts of life-maintaining heat-energy. Gradually, the routine feels less uncomfortable. Pat nudges the altitude hold on the autopilot up to thirty-four-thousand feet. The higher the altitude, the better our fuel mileage – and the sooner we will be able to pick up the radio navigation beacon from Goose Bay.

Also, the higher we fly, the quieter it gets and the lonelier it feels. The lonelier it feels, the greater the spiritual experience. It's just simple working-class Relativity.

Gradually, however, right at the apex of our solitude drama, off to the right-front of the plane, at our two o'clock, a spooky curtain of color slowly emerges from the darkness. It then explodes rapidly over the whole dim western sky. It's a blooming of soft-blue/greenish curtains – an *aurora borealis*. It spreads rapidly to the east across our path. Then it spreads even further to the west–northwest as well. It feels only minutes ahead of us. Now it's spreading and thickening to block our route south. There will be no getting around this thing. We're going to have to punch through it.

On the other hand, I'm wondering if it might perpetually recede away from us like the rainbow you can never catch. Who knows? I check the radios and navigation instruments to see if I can pick up any electronic transmission anomalies. This should be a good experiment, but I detect absolutely no reactions.

The heavenly display recalls a discussion Pat and I had a month ago with some Georgia Tech geophysicists. We were discussing solar storms and the effect they may have on the earth's magnetic flux. This makes me wonder what effect this auroral display is having on the magnetic compass heading we're following so faithfully. Can the aurora borealis cause *magnetic* bearing aberrations? I think the geophysicist at Tech said *no*, but I can't really recall the science behind them. I've read that the Northern Lights are the consequence of solar winds blowing out from the sun, thus energizing the earth's magnetic field as it bends vertically into the Magnetic Poles. But maybe this cause and effect is the other way around. Right now, it doesn't make any difference. Whatever it is, it's all above and dead ahead of us. The scale of its stage set is making us infinitesimal.

As we approach the nearest drape, the luminosity goes from benign shimmers across the horizon to brighter, center-stage lighting. Then the main act emerges right in front of us. Directly in our path are three receding layers of heavy, vertical curtains. Their curvilinear upper edge is blurry and the hemline almost has an edge to it. The color is a monochrome pale-lime-green with a soot-black backdrop that's loosely scattered with the sparkle-dust of stars shining through it. The radiance of the aurora is getting a little stronger, but it's still not bright enough to read by. There is no conversation going on inside the plane. Talking would be like whispering secrets during a Pope's sermon.

As we penetrate the hemline of the first drape, Pat dims the lights of the cockpit instrument panel. Then, so we can look up between the curtains, he switches the autopilot off and rolls the plane ninety degrees up on its left wing. I get to look up first. To maintain positive G's, he must bank the plane into a half circle to the left. He holds this high-G position for four or five seconds, then whips the plane (more abruptly than I think he should) to the right so *he* can look with the other wing up. We're carving *high-altitude S-turns through the Northern Lights.* Hot-dogging near the "coffin corner" in the middle of the night is an incautious exercise at best. But there really is no other way to see everything.[25]

---

[25] Stall speed decreases with altitude. Consequently, to fly higher and higher, a plane must fly faster and faster. At some point, the

We then fly under the bottom hem of the second skirt. I look for auroral sparkles to flow over the wings like the contrails of World War II bombers. There are none. We must be below the actual source of luminescence. Then, in a blink, the third skirt comes up. Another blink and we're through it. Then it's all behind us. It was a magic moment of one of Mother Nature's most exhilarating cosmic introductions. She appeared across our midnight path, teased us with her swirling skirts, gave us a peek, and then shooed us out the back door like snickering schoolboys caught trying to play grown-up pranks.

The incredible beauty and grandeur of what we just participated in may or may not serve as compensation for the fierce wind demonstration that she showed us on the ice cap not 24 hours ago. Personally, I think not. But when toying with the mysteries of the Universe, the temptation to suggest compensation for the powerful forces of nature is only the blameless ambition of a human spirit left only with the ignorance of heavenly awe.

No matter how you express it, this final salute tonight certainly smacks of the theatrical. If it had come with a thunderous musical background of lyrical violins, blaring trumpets, swooning trombones, and crashing cymbals, it might have suggested a heroic ending to an epic Arctic tale.

But this flight home is not a final curtain. This event we just flew through is only the fanfare to the ending of a beginning chapter in a story of purpose and determination. And, of course, there is also the lingering image I think I saw of Mother Nature waving her hanky with a "Toodle-loo, boys. See y'all later."

---

limitations of power will meet the higher stall speed, and the plane will then fall out of the sky. In aviation jargon, this is called the *coffin corner*.

At the end of this four-hour flight, we hit Goose Bay spot-on. After we land, I find and remove my sleeping bag that I, whilst criticizing a soft whistler, had errantly stuffed in front of the main heater vent in the cabin. We refuel the plane, wolf down cellophane packets of salty-sugary junk food, set the cabin temperature to quiet perfection, and wend our way home at half the speed of sound in quiet, elegant, thermal comfort. Rajani flies this leg.

As we fly the rest of the night and half of the next day, I have plenty of time to mentally compose tonight's closing scene for this, our second failed Greenland expedition.

Imagine framing both sides of an extraordinarily starry skyscape mural with multiple layers of pale, lime-green, translucent, deep-folded drapery. Then, written between the gauzed proscenium, in a large wispy-white font, the auroral drape reads:

John Gillespie Magee, Jr.
High Flight

"Oh, I have slipped the surly bonds of earth,
And danced the skies on laughter-silvered wings;
Sunward I've climbed and joined the tumbling mirth of
sun-split clouds -
and done a hundred things You have not dreamed of -
wheeled and soared and swung high in the sunlit silence.
Hovering there I've chased the shouting wind along
and flung my eager craft through footless halls of air.

"Up, up the long delirious burning blue
I've topped the wind-swept heights with easy grace,
where never lark, or even eagle, flew;
and, while with silent, lifting mind I've trod
the high untrespassed sanctity of space,
put out my hand and touched the face of God."

Photo Credits:

Number	Page	Subject	Photographer
1.	Cover	Roll the Pole	R. Taylor
2.	2	R. Taylor	Army chum
3.	10	R. Taylor	Nancy Mitchell
4.	22	Mooney Sketch	R. Taylor
5.	53	R. Taylor/N. Mitchell	Friend
6.	84	Bay Bridge	State of MD
7.	138	Cessna 185	R. Taylor
8.	166	Polar Trip Maps	R. Taylor
9.	170	Taylor & Epps	Friend
10.	172	Lost Squadron	US Gov't
11.	174	1981 Camp	R. Taylor
12.	176	Ice Berg	R. Taylor
13.	178	R. Taylor	Lou Sapienza
14.	179	Believe it or Not	R. Taylor
15.	180	Epps & Taylor	Lou Sapienza
16.	181	Sketch	R. Taylor
17.	183	Exploders Club	R. Taylor
18.	184	P-38	Lou Sapienza
19.	184	Tail Section	Lou Sapienza
20.	185	Glacier Girl	Cornelius Brown
21.	186	Class Picture	Lou Sapienza
22.	187	Helicopter	Lou Sapienza
23.	189	Doug Epps	Lou Sapienza
24.	205	DC-3	Lou Sapienza
25.	227	You Haven't Failed	R. Taylor
26.	231	R. Taylor	Lou Sapienza

RICHARD L. TAYLOR, Jr. is an Architect, a Pilot and a Fellow in both the Explorers Club and the American Institute of Architects.

For diversion, he races vintage sports cars and motorcycles.

For ballast, there is real estate development, beekeeping, writing and family duties that seem to fill the bill.

www.ingramcontent.com/pod-product-compliance
Lightning Source LLC
Chambersburg PA
CBHW041958090426
42811CB00030B/1950/J